# SNACKS & GAMES

A Fun, Lesson-based Snack & Game for Each Lesson!

NexGen® is an imprint of
Cook Communications Ministries, Colorado Springs, CO
Cook Communications, Paris Ontario
Kingsway Communications, Eastbourne, England

NOAH'S PARK® CHILDREN'S CHURCH SNACKS & GAMES (Red Edition)
© 2007 by Cook Communications Ministries
4050 Lee Vance View
Colorado Springs, CO 80918-7100

First printing 2007
Printed in the United States of America

1 2 3 4 5 6 7 8 9 10 Printing/Year 11 10 09 08 07

Editor:                    Carol Pitts
Contributing Writers:      Mary Brite, Judy Gillispie, Karen James,
                           Gail Rohlfing, Scott Stewart, Nancy Sutton
Interior Design:           Mike Riester
Cover Design:              Todd Mock
Illustrations:             Aline Heiser, Chris Sharp

ISBN: 978-0-781444-91-0                                        105094

# TABLE OF CONTENTS

**Introduction**    6

### Unit 1 *Creation*

**Lesson 1**
Snack: *Star Cookies*    7
E-Game: *The Creator Said*    7
P-Game: *Daytime and Nighttime Toss*    8
**Lesson 2**
Snack: *Useful Plant Snacks*    9
E-Game: *Water Relays*    9
P-Game: *Plant Hide-and-Seek*    10
**Lesson 3**
Snack: *Bugs and Stuff*    11
E-Game: *Animal Tag*    11
P-Game: *Animal Relay*    12
**Lesson 4**
Snack: *Friendly Snacks*    13
E-Game: *Creative Obstacle Course*    13
P-Game: *God Made . . .*    14

### Unit 2 *God's Promises*

**Lesson 5**
Snack: *Fruit Garden*    15
E-Game: *Listen Up*    15
P-Game: *May I, Please?*    16
**Lesson 6**
Snack: *Noah's Ark Snacks*    17
E-Game: *Ark Builder Obstacle Course*    17
P-Game: *Into the Ark*    18
**Lesson 7**
Snack: *Shady Blankets*    19
E-Game: *Promise Hunt*    19
P-Game: *As Many Stars in the Heavens*    20
**Lesson 8**
Snack: *Traveling Snacks*    21
E-Game: *Camel Packin' Relays*    21
P-Game: *Traveling Game*    22

### Unit 3 *The Exodus*

**Lesson 9**
Snack: *Burning Bushes*    23
E-Game: *Here I Am*    23
P-Game: *Helping Chairs*    24
**Lesson 10**
Snack: *Celery Frogs*    25
E-Game: *"Keep Trying" Charades*    25
P-Game: *Ball Test*    26
**Lesson 11**
Snack: *Passover Snack*    27
E-Game: *Lamb Tag*    27
P-Game: *Find the Passover Dessert*    28
**Lesson 12**
Snack: *Celebration Snacks*    29
E-Game: *Red Sea Water*    29
P-Game: *Through the Sea*    30
**Lesson 13**
Snack: *Snacks from Our Talents*    31
E-Game: *Talent Races*    31
P-Game: *Offering Relay*    32

### Unit 4 *Conquering the Promised Land*

**Lesson 14**
Snack: *God's Good Food*    33
E-Game: *Going to the Promised Land*    33
P-Game: *Spying Out the Land Relay*    34
**Lesson 15**
Snack: *Jericho Rubble*    35
E-Game: *Wall of Jerhicho March*    35
P-Game: *Marching Around Jericho*    36
**Lesson 16**
Snack: *Undercover Snacks*    37
E-Game: *You Can't Fool Me*    37
P-Game: *Tricky Tag*    38
**Lesson 17**
Snack: *Big and Small Snacks*    39
E-Game: *The Day the Kids Stood Still*    39
P-Game: *Go! The Sun Is Shining*    40

### Unit 5 *Choosing and Losing*

**Lesson 18**
Snack: *Good Chocolate Chip Cookies*    41
E-Game: *Samuel Says*    41

# TABLE OF CONTENTS

P-Game: *Calling Game*     42

**Unit 5 Choosing and Losing**

**Lesson 19**
Snack: *Choices*     43
E-Game: *The King Wants to Know*     43
P-Game: *Donkeys or a Crown?*     44

**Lesson 20**
Snack: *Power Snacks*     45
E-Game: *What Time Is It, Goliath?*     45
P-Game: *What Should I Take to Fight?*     46

**Lesson 21**
Snack: *Thankful-Heart Sandwiches*     47
E-Game: *Cat and Mouse*     47
P-Game: *Happy/Sad Game*     48

**Unit 6 Royalty and Loyalty**

**Lesson 22**
Snack: *Friendship Snack*     49
E-Game: *Smiles, Handshakes, or Hugs*     49
P-Game: *Elbow to Elbow—Friend to Friend* 50

**Lesson 23**
Snack: *A Snack for David's Army*     51
E-Game: *Finding Saul's Spear*     51
P-Game: *Tag a King*     52

**Lesson 24**
Snack: *Lemonade and Donuts*     53
E-Game: *David and the Amalekites*     53
P-Game: *Can You Help Me Find My
        Brother (or Sister)?*     54

**Lesson 25**
Snack: *Celebration Cookies*     55
E-Game: *David's Celebration Dance*     55
P-Game: *The King's Parade*     56

**Unit 7 Wise to Advise**

**Lesson 26**
Snack: *ABCs of Wisdom*     57
E-Game: *What Would I Want?*     57
P-Game: *Follow the King*     58

**Lesson 27**
Snack: *Where's My Snack?*     59
E-Game: *Who Did It?*     59
P-Game: *King Solomon, May I?*     60

**Lesson 28**
Snack: *Build a Snack*     61
E-Game: *Temple Workers Mix-up*     61
P-Game: *Building the Temple*     62

**Lesson 29**
Snack: *Be Wise Snack*     63
E-Game: *Come, Be Wise*     63
P-Game: *Jeroboam Tag*     64

**Unit 8 A Time for Decision**

**Lesson 30**
Snack: *Apple Consequence Snack*     65
E-Game: *What's My Consequence?*     65
P-Game: *Shelter-by-the-Brook Relay*     66

**Lesson 31**
Snack: *Elijah's Drought Food*     67
E-Game: *Elijah's Bread and Water*     67
P-Game: *Baking Bread*     68

**Lesson 32**
Snack: *Prayer Pretzels*     69
E-Game: *Answer Me*     69
P-Game: *Listen to the Whisper*     70

**Lesson 33**
Snack: *Big "G" Snacks*     71
E-Game: *Follow Me*     71
P-Game: *Building-Block Altar*     72

**Lesson 34**
Snack: *Comfort Food*     73
E-Game: *Who Cared for Me?*     73
P-Game: *Where Is God?*     74

**Lesson 35**
Snack: *Disappearing Snack*     75
E-Game: *Two-Kid Tag*     75
P-Game: *Coat Tag*     76

# TABLE OF CONTENTS

### Unit 9 *A Time for Courage*

**Lesson 36**

| | |
|---|---|
| Snack: *Guess How Many* | 77 |
| E-Game: *In-the-Dark Walk* | 77 |
| P-Game: *Crown Freeze Tag* | 78 |

**Lesson 37**

| | |
|---|---|
| Snack: *Fiery Snack Scene* | 79 |
| E-Game: *Following God through the Noise* | 79 |
| P-Game: *Touch the King* | 80 |

**Lesson 38**

| | |
|---|---|
| Snack: *Finger Writing* | 81 |
| E-Game: *Secret Message Relay* | 81 |
| P-Game: *Party Relay* | 82 |

**Lesson 39**

| | |
|---|---|
| Snack: *Popcorn Prayer Snack* | 83 |
| E-Game: *The King's New Laws* | 83 |
| P-Game: *Lion to Lion* | 84 |

### Unit 10 *The Person Christ Needs*

**Lesson 40**

| | |
|---|---|
| Snack: *Colorful Treats* | 85 |
| E-Game: *Escape from Damascus* | 85 |
| P-Game: *Sunglass Pass* | 86 |

**Lesson 41**

| | |
|---|---|
| Snack: *Journey Snacks* | 87 |
| E-Game: *Walk-Ride-Sail Relay* | 87 |
| P-Game: *Willing Heart Simon Says* | 88 |

**Lesson 42**

| | |
|---|---|
| Snack: *Coin-Shaped Treats* | 89 |
| E-Game: *Roll It* | 89 |
| P-Game: *Gathering Gifts Relay* | 90 |

**Lesson 43**

| | |
|---|---|
| Snack: *Pudding Power* | 91 |
| E-Game: *Bubble Dodge* | 91 |
| P-Game: *Hug Time* | 92 |

**Lesson 44**

| | |
|---|---|
| Snack: *Stick Together* | 93 |
| E-Game: *Throw It Overboard!* | 93 |
| P-Game: *Ship in a Storm* | 94 |

### Unit 11 *Jesus the Savior*

**Lesson 45**

| | |
|---|---|
| Snack: *Sweet Scrolls* | 95 |
| E-Game: *Scroll Search* | 95 |
| P-Game: *God's Promises* | 96 |

**Lesson 46**

| | |
|---|---|
| Snack: *Bible-Time Foods* | 97 |
| E-Game: *Gift Pyramid Relay* | 97 |
| P-Game: *Angel, Mary, Joseph* | 98 |

**Lesson 47**

| | |
|---|---|
| Snack: *Animal Crackers* | 99 |
| E-Game: *Good News Relay* | 99 |
| P-Game: *Shepherds Go to Bethlehem* | 100 |

**Lesson 48**

| | |
|---|---|
| Snack: *Christmas Cookies* | 101 |
| E-Game: *Wise Man Caravan* | 101 |
| P-Game: *Follow the Star* | 102 |

### Unit 12 *Jesus the Sacrifice*

**Lesson 49**

| | |
|---|---|
| Snack: *Never-Ending Treats* | 103 |
| E-Game: *Hoop Race* | 103 |
| P-Game: *"God Loves You" Train* | 104 |

**Lesson 50**

| | |
|---|---|
| Snack: *"J" Is for Jesus* | 105 |
| E-Game: *Jesus Knows You* | 105 |
| P-Game: *Call-a-Name Tag* | 106 |

**Lesson 51**

| | |
|---|---|
| Snack: *Cross Creations* | 107 |
| E-Game: *Forgiven Tag* | 107 |
| P-Game: *God Forgives Bridge* | 108 |

**Lesson 52**

| | |
|---|---|
| Snack: *Sweet Spices* | 109 |
| E-Game: *Run to the Tomb* | 109 |
| P-Game: *Angel Surprise* | 110 |

**Lesson 53**

| | |
|---|---|
| Snack: *Cheesy Books* | 111 |
| E-Game: *Obstacles on the Road to Emmaus* | 111 |
| P-Game: *The Emmaus Road* | 112 |

# INTRODUCTION

The snacks and games provided in this book are coordinated with the lessons in the Noah's Park *Leader's Guide*. These pages are reproducible so that you can give each Park Patrol member or leader involved with snacks or games a copy for the individual lessons. You will notice that for each lesson the snack suggestion and elementary game are listed on one page and that the same snack suggestion and the preschool game are listed on the back of that page.

You may choose to keep all the children together during Snack Shack or you may separate the children into their age-appropriate groups before the snack. Use the method that works best for your situation. This may be determined by the number of children participating, by your room arrangement, or other factors.

When the children arrive for Children's Church the first week, take time to have the parents fill out a registration form. (Your Children's Ministry Director may have a form that is used for this purpose.) Be sure to have parents list any food allergies and keep this information in the classroom so that you can refer to it. Also be sure to have the parents indicate any physical limitations that might be affected by the games (such as asthma, etc.).

Basic supplies you should keep on hand for snacks:
· Napkins
· Cups
· Paper plates
· Paper towels
· Plastic spoons and forks
· Craft sticks to spread (instead of plastic knives)
· Crackers (for children who have allergies and cannot eat the day's snack suggestion)
· Sponges
· Disposable wipes
· Dishpan and soap
· Resealable plastic bags (to send snacks home that the children may not finish)

# LESSON 1 SNACK:
# Star Cookies

**Supplies:** Sugar cookie recipe of your choosing, star-shaped cookie cutters, yellow decorator's frosting, snack-size resealable plastic bags, plates, napkins, wet wipes for cleanup

**Preparation:** Make two star-shaped cookies per child. Place a tablespoon of yellow decorator's frosting in a bottom corner of each resealable plastic bag. Squeeze the air from each bag as you seal it.

**Directions:** Give each child one or two cookies. Snip one-eighth inch from the corner nearest the frosting in each resealable bag. Give each child a bag of frosting. Tell the children to squeeze the frosting through the open corner to decorate their star cookies. Let them enjoy decorating and eating!

Note: For a quicker alternative that doesn't involve baking or frosting, you might substitute chocolate sandwich cookies (for night), vanilla cookies (for day), and star-shaped crackers.

# LESSON 1 ELEMENTARY GAME:
# The Creator Said

**Supplies:** None

**Directions:** Have the children stand up and spread out so they have room to move. Explain that when you say, "The Creator said, 'Let there be *earth*,'" they must turn around once. If you say *"sun"* rather than earth, they put arms overhead in a big arch touching fingertips. For *moon*, the children should put their hands up with fingers spread wide beside their smiling faces. For *stars*, they open and close both hands quickly and repeatedly.

Those doing wrong actions move to the back, but continue to play. Encourage careful listening and begin slowly. Show the correct actions at first. Increase the challenge and speed. Give alternative instructions and/or different accompanying actions.

If your children are older or catch on quickly, you might add this element: If you do not say, "The Creator said," kids should stand still. Invite a Park Patrol member to take your place and see if he or she can trick the children—and you!

# LESSON 1 PRESCHOOL GAME:
# Daytime and Nighttime Toss

**Supplies:** Three pieces of black paper, three pieces of yellow paper, tape, beanbag

**Preparation:** Tape the six pieces of paper in a line, alternating the black and white papers. Put a line of tape six inches in front of the line of papers.

**Directions: We learned today that God made daytime and nighttime as part of His creation plan. You will take turns tossing the beanbag. If the beanbag lands on a white paper, tell us something you do in the daytime. If it lands on a dark paper, tell something you do in the nighttime.**

Have the children stand behind the tape line and take turns tossing the beanbag and then telling an activity. Older preschoolers could hop from paper to paper until they reach the beanbag.

## LESSON 2 SNACK:
# Useful Plant Snacks

**Supplies:** A variety of snack foods made from plants, such as carrots, celery, raisins, orange wedges, crackers, potato chips, pretzels, sunflower seeds, plates or napkins

**Directions:** Put snack foods made from plants on plates in the center of your snack table. For the sake of allergies, avoid nuts.

Let a few children at a time politely help themselves to one or two of any of the "plants" on the table until all have some snacks. While the children are "grazing," talk with them about the parts of plants they're eating. Reinforce how your snack is an example of the useful and beautiful world God created.

## LESSON 2 ELEMENTARY GAME:
# Water Relays

**Supplies:** Water, two buckets or basins per team, paper cups, towels for cleanup

**Directions:** Divide the children into teams. Fill one bucket for each team with an equal amount of water and place it at your starting line. Have each team form a line behind a bucket. Place an empty bucket for each team some distance from the starting line. Give the first person in each line a cup.

Tell the children that when you give the signal, the first person in each line fills the cup about three-fourths full of water, goes to the empty bucket, empties the cup into it, and carries the empty cup back to the next person in line. Each player in line repeats the relay. After all complete the relay, the entire team sits down.

Assign the Park Patrol with Noah's Park puppets to referee and do cleanup. See which team can have the most water end up in their end-line bucket.

As time permits, run other water relays where the children walk backward or sidestep.

## LESSON 2 PRESCHOOL GAME:
# Plant Hide-and-Seek

**Supplies:** Artificial plants, flowers, and fruit (at least one item for each child)

**Directions:** Show the plants and fruits to the children. **God made plants. Some are flowers. Some grow fruit on them.** Have the Park Patrol hide all the plants, flowers, and fruit in the room while the children cover their eyes. When everything has been hidden, ask the children to find the plants. When a plant is found, the child finding it should call out, "God made plants. God made (plant, flower, or fruit.)."

Have the Park Patrol hide the plants again to continue the game. For older preschoolers, have them name the type of fruit that is found.

# LESSON 3 SNACK:
# Bugs and Stuff

**Supplies:** Celery sticks, cream cheese, raisins, sunflower seeds, baby carrots, banana slices, small candy-coated chocolate candies, round crackers, plates, napkins, plastic knives

**Directions:** Set out plates of celery sticks, baby carrots, raisins, sunflower seeds, small candy-coated chocolate candies, banana slices, round crackers, and packages of cream cheese. Give each child a plastic butter knife, napkin, and small plate.

Show the children how to spread cheese in a celery stick or on a round cracker and then use the small items to make Ants on a Log, Bugs on a Rock, or animal faces.

It might be necessary to assign a Park Patrol member to hand out the chocolate candies so each child gets only a few.

For a quick and easy alternative, provide animal crackers and fish-shaped crackers.

# LESSON 3 ELEMENTARY GAME:
# Animal Tag

**Supplies:** Optional: masking tape

**Directions:** Have the children form teams. Each team selects an animal name—preferably an animal that runs fast and is easy to mimic during a tag game! Identify boundaries and a "cage" where each team will take those it tags out of the game. If playing indoors, you might put masking tape on the floor to identify the cages.

Children move around like their team animal. Kangaroos hop and jump, elephants hang and swing their arms, horses gallop, and rabbits hop or run in zig zag patterns. Teammates work together to tag opponents and escort them to the team's cage. Players in an opponent's cage must remain there until tagged and released by one of their own teammates. If any team manages to capture all of an opposing team's players, end the game, choose different animals, and play again.

Park Patrol members can be officials and also remind kids to keep moving in ways that mimic their team animal name.

# LESSON 3 PRESCHOOL GAME:
# Animal Relay

**Supplies:** None

**Directions:** Divide the children into two equal groups. Stand at one end of the classroom to call out animal names. Have the first person in each line move toward you, imitating that animal. Once they reach, they turn around and go to the back of their line. You may want to let the children suggest different animals to use.

**God made animals. Let's move like animals.** Some ideas to begin the game with are:

**God made elephants.**

**God made monkeys.**

**God made horses.**

**God made frogs.**

## LESSON 4 SNACK:
# Friendly Snacks

**Supplies:** Bowls of sunflower seeds, tiny pretzels, small crackers, sesame sticks, raisins, dried fruit, other bite-size snack foods, plates or napkins, serving spoons

**Directions:** Have the children wash their hands. Provide large bowls of sunflower nuts, tiny pretzels, small crackers, sesame sticks, raisins, other dried fruit pieces, and other bite-size snack foods. Include a serving spoon in each bowl. Pass the bowls and let each group decide together what they want to use in their own creative snack mix. Once everyone is served, each group enjoys its snack creation.

## LESSON 4 ELEMENTARY GAME:
# Creative Obstacle Course

**Supplies:** Blocks, chairs, trash cans, string, tape, and other objects and supplies available in the classroom

**Directions:** Divide the children into small teams. If possible, include a Park Patrol member on each team. Tell the teams they will have two minutes to plan one creative part of an obstacle course from the materials you provide. They might stack blocks to hop over, arrange chairs to wind through, stretch out string to crawl under, or anything else that comes to their minds. Encourage creative use of the materials you offer. Assign each team a part of the room to build in.

When time is up, ask each team to tell what they made and demonstrate how to get through it. Then line everyone up to go through every obstacle on the course. Reinforce that we are creative because God created us to be like Him.

As a supply-free alternative, have each small group "make up" their own new game. Encourage them to build on an existing game, such as tag, with their own unique twist to it or rules for it. Each team may briefly demonstrate their game for the others, as there won't be time to play every team's game.

## LESSON 4 PRESCHOOL GAME:
# God Made . . .

**Supplies:** None

**Directions:** Play this version of "Simon Says" to help children explore God's special creation of people. Have the children stand in a line in front of you. When you say, "God made people. People have (part of the body)," the children should point to that body part. **God made people. People have** (hands, eyes, ears, nose, legs, arms, etc.**).**

## LESSON 5 SNACK:
# Fruit Garden

**Supplies:** Apple, pear, and banana slices; orange sections; pineapple chunks; raisins and other dried fruits; plates; napkins; plastic forks or toothpicks

**Preparation:** Prepare fruits and place on serving plates.

**Directions:** Provide each child with a plate, napkin, and plastic fork or several toothpicks. Set out the fruit trays and let children choose fruits to move onto their plates and enjoy. Remind the children to use their forks or toothpicks rather than fingers to remove the fruits from the serving tray.

As a quick and easy alternative, provide packaged fruit snacks in fruit shapes.

## LESSON 5 ELEMENTARY GAME:
# Listen Up

**Supplies:** None

**Directions:** Have the children stand against a far wall and face you. **Listen and do only my directions that include the word "go." If you disobey, you must return to your starting spot. Let's see how quickly you can reach me by listening and following directions.**

Begin with easy and slow directions such as, **Step forward three times, go. Turn in a circle, go.** And intersperse directions without the word "go": **Take a giant step.** Point out children who make "good decisions" by listening carefully. Let Park Patrol members listen and watch to help you keep track of who is obeying.

Gradually increase the complexity, speed, and challenge of instructions. For example, tell them to do something and don't say, "Go," but you do the action. Or give a direction and say, "Go," but do a wrong action and watch if they copy you. Try multi step directions such as **jump, sit, stand, turn around, and go.** Watch that the children don't confuse the order.

The round ends when a child reaches you. As time permits, have the children return to the starting line and play again.

## LESSON 5 PRESCHOOL GAME:
# May I, Please?

**Supplies:** None

**Directions:** This version of "Mother, May I?" helps children work on their listening skills. **Adam and Eve should have listened carefully to what God said and remembered it. Let's practice how well we listen while we play our game. I'll tell you how to move to me. You'll ask, "May I, please?" If I say, "Yes, you may," then you can move. If I answer some other way, stay still.**

Have the children stand at the other end of the room and take turns while you give instructions such as, "Walk forward two steps" or "Hop five times." Play until a child reaches you.

## LESSON 6 SNACK:
# Noah's Ark Snacks

**Supplies:** Chocolate pudding, blue gelatin, celery, carrots, pretzel sticks, O-shaped dry cereal, chocolate chips, marshmallows, animal crackers, plates, plastic spoons, napkins

**Directions:** Show the children the containers of mud pudding, floodwater gelatin, gopher wood celery and carrots, pretzel stick pegs, cereal lifepreservers, chocolate raindrops, marshmallow clouds, and animal crackers. Let the Park Patrol help serve to avoid spills and ensure that children don't choose too much sugar.

## LESSON 6 ELEMENTARY GAME:
# Ark Builder Obstacle Course

**Supplies:** Sheet, round trash cans

**Directions:** Lead your class through this lively obstacle course of pretend ark building. Have the children work in pairs. Demonstrate each section of the obstacle course described below. Then line up the pairs and send them through about 15 seconds after the pair in front of them. Station Park Patrol members along the course to remind the children what they are to do at each section.

Dragging Logs: Each person in a pair grabs one end of a rolled-up sheet and plays a brief tug-of-war. If you'd like, have a pair on each end of the sheet.

Cutting Wood: A pair holds hands as if shaking hands but saws their arms back and forth. If you'd like, they may do this while walking one lap around the room.

Pounding Pegs: Pairs hit one fist to the other person's palm, back and forth. (Remind the children not to pound hard enough to hurt.) Again, the pair may do this while taking a lap around the room.

Sealing Wood: Both players in a pair face a long wall (the ark) and sidestep down the length of it. As they do this, they pretend to hold a bucket in one hand and paint up and down with a brush with the other hand.

Loading Supplies: Each player in a pair rolls a trash can along the floor to race to an end point and back. If you'd like, have a pair roll one trash can to race another pair.

Leading Animals: One player in a pair leads the other player (whose eyes are closed) one lap around the room.

# LESSON 6 PRESCHOOL GAME:
# Into the Ark

**Supplies:** Masking tape

**Preparation:** Use masking tape to make a boat-shaped outline on the floor.

**Directions: God sent all different kinds of animals to go on Noah's boat.** Give each child an animal name. Set up a starting point and a simple path around the room. Have the children move like their assigned animal to get in the boat. You may want to let the children choose their own types of animals.

# LESSON 7 SNACK:
# Shady Blankets

**Supplies:** Blanket, snack crackers, cheese, baby carrots, plates, napkins

**Directions:** To begin snack time, play the role of Abraham and sit on a blanket on the floor as Abraham. Have the Park Patrol bring the children and tell them to stand near the blanket. Stand up, bow to the children, and invite them to sit on the blanket. Then serve the children plates, napkins, snack crackers, bite-size cheese, baby carrots, and other snack items the children will enjoy. Let all sit on the blanket to enjoy the snack.

# LESSON 7 ELEMENTARY GAME:
# Promise Hunt

**Supplies:** Notepaper or scrap paper, pencil, various paper bags, plastic food containers, boxes, Bibles, (optional: bite-size candy bars)

**Preparation:** Write a sequence of treasure hunt clues with promises (below) on notepaper or squares of scrap paper. Place all but the first clue in bags, containers, and boxes, and hide them around the room. You might include candy bars in the final bag.

Promises and clue suggestion (adapt to fit your room):

**Look in your teacher's pocket.**

**God promises to love us: Isaiah 54:10. Look under something you sit on.**

**God promises to forgive us: 1 John 1:9. Look up in a tall place.**

**God promises to save us: Ephesians 2:8. Look where you leave the room.**

**God promises His blessing: Ephesians 1:3. Look in a new bag in our room.**

**God promises to give us peace: John 14:27. Look inside a special Book.**

**God promises joy: John 15:11. Look near our music.**

**God promises to be with us: Matthew 28:20. Look among our supplies.**

**Directions:** Tell the children to work together to find "promise treasures." Read the first clue and let the children begin. When they find each one, someone reads it and holds onto it until the end of the game. When finished, let volunteers look up the verses and read them aloud for the class.

## LESSON 7 PRESCHOOL GAME:
# As Many Stars in the Heavens

**Supplies:** Paper stars, masking tape

**Preparation:** Cut enough paper stars so that each child has one.

**Directions:** Choose one child to be IT. The other children will be stars. Tape a paper star on the front of each child. **God promised Abraham that there would be lots of children in His family—as many children as there are stars in the sky! It would take a long, long time.**

**Let's pretend to be the stars in the sky. When the person who is IT taps you, freeze and say, "God keeps all His promises."**

Let the children move around the game area. IT tries to tag the "stars." When a "star" is touched, he or she stops moving and says, "God keeps all His promises." The tagged stars need to stay where they are until all the stars have been tagged. The last "star" to be tagged becomes the new IT.

## LESSON 8 SNACK:

# Traveling Snacks

**Supplies:** Snack mix (raisins, sunflower seeds, tiny pretzels, sesame sticks, fish-shaped crackers, candy-coated chocolates, etc.), resealable plastic bags, picnic basket or knapsack, napkins, picnic blanket

**Preparation:** Choose snack mix items and put them in resealable plastic bags, one handful for each child. Put the bags in a picnic basket or knapsack with napkins.

Tell the children that you are leading them on a journey. Remind them that people in today's Bible story went on a journey too. Carrying the picnic basket and blanket, lead the children on a trip around the room, ending at a spot for snacking. Lay out the blanket for the children to sit on. After the snack, have the children put their napkins and empty bags in the basket and follow you as you lead them on their journey to Campsite Capers.

## LESSON 8 ELEMENTARY GAME:

# Camel Packin' Relays

**Supplies:** (Per team) trash can, socks, shoes, stuffed grocery bags, hats, toothbrush, water bottles, cups, paper plates, spoons, string or rope, other assorted traveling items

**Preparation:** Try out the game ahead of time to figure out how much stuff will fit on top of the upside-down trash cans. Make sure they are full with a chance of things falling off if not carefully placed. Compile an identical set of objects for each team.

**Directions:** Divide the children into teams for a relay. Line up the teams on a starting line. For each team, place a trash can upside-down at an end point. This will be the camel. Place the other materials on the start line for each team.

At your signal, the first player on each team picks up an object from his team's pile, runs it to the camel (trash can), places it where it won't fall off, and runs back to tag the next player. Team members run objects to their camel until all the team's objects are loaded and ready to travel.

Any objects that fall off the camel must be returned to the start line by a runner who goes only to get fallen objects. Another runner will carry fallen objects and try again to place them on the camel. Speed and good packing are both important to win. May the best camel packers win!

# LESSON 8 PRESCHOOL GAME:
# Traveling Game

**Supplies:** Four classroom chairs

**Preparation:** Place the chairs in a small circle at one end of your game area to form a well. Ask a Park Patrol helper to pretend to be Rebekah.

**Directions:** Gather the children together at the end of your game area opposite the well. Have them stand in a line behind you.

**Let's pretend to travel with Abraham's servant. We can travel on our camels to the well.** Gallop in a zigzag path to the well. Have the children follow you. Once you are at the well, pretend to dismount the camels while Rebekah pretends to give them water.

**Let's go back to find Isaac. This time our camels will take baby steps.** Walk back to the beginning using baby steps.

Continue traveling back and forth to the well using a different movement each time. Children may suggest hopping, walking, marching, and so forth.

## LESSON 9 SNACK:
# Burning Bushes

**Supplies:** Crackers, cheese spread, broccoli trees, baby carrots, pretzel sticks, pretzel logs, plates, napkins, plastic knives

**Directions:** Let the children choose a favorite food to use as the trunks of their bushes—broccoli trees, baby carrots, or crackers. Then let them spread cheese on the trunk and stick in pretzel sticks as branches. Some children might prefer the fiery orange carrot sticks as burning branches. Or you might use pretzel logs as the trunks and small pretzel sticks as the branches. Of course Moses' burning bush wasn't consumed, but these will be!

## LESSON 9 ELEMENTARY GAME:
# Here I Am

**Supplies:** Blindfold

Use a large area safe for a blindfolded child to walk through. Ask a volunteer to be blindfolded. The remaining children quietly scatter around the blindfolded person and freeze. The blindfolded person calls a child's name twice, just as God called Moses twice. The one whose name was called says, "Here I am." The blindfolded volunteer listens and moves to tag the person whose name he or she called. The child whose name was called may not move, and the blindfolded child must work around any others in his or her way.

Select another volunteer to be blindfolded and repeat the game.

## LESSON 9 PRESCHOOL GAME:
# Helping Chairs

**Supplies:** Chair for each child, Noah's Park CD, CD player

**Preparation:** Set up the chairs in a circle with the seats facing out. Have one for each child.

**Directions:** Have the children sit in the chairs. **When you hear the music, stand up and walk around the circle of chairs. When the music stops, help each other find a place to sit.** Play the Unit Song, "God's Already There," stopping the music after 15 seconds. Let all the children sit down. Then remove two chairs and continue playing the game. When the music stops, the children will have to help find ways for everyone to sit down. (Sitting on laps is an easy way.) Continue playing and stopping the music, removing one or two chairs each time the music is played. Play the game until only a couple of chairs are left.

# LESSON 10 SNACK:
# Celery Frogs

**Supplies:** Pretzel sticks, celery sticks, cream cheese or sunflower seed butter, plastic knives, plates, napkins

**Directions:** Have each child spread cream cheese or sunflower seed butter in a celery stick. The children then turn it upside-down and push two long pretzel sticks into it near the end to serve as rear frog legs. They break another pretzel stick in half and push each piece into the celery on each side about an inch from the top for front legs. Let the frogs hop into the children's mouths.

# LESSON 10 ELEMENTARY GAME:
# "Keep Trying" Charades

**Supplies:** Index cards, pencil

**Preparation:** Write the statements below on separate index cards. You may add more sentences as you wish.

You keep trying to get a mean kid to stop hitting you on the playground.

You keep trying to do a math problem and can't get it right.

You keep trying to get your younger brother to stop bothering you.

You keep trying to get a classmate to stop telling you to cheat on a test.

You keep trying to walk up a long, steep hill.

You keep trying to carry a very heavy box.

Divide the children into small teams. You may assign a Park Patrol member to each team. Give each team a skit card. Tell the teams to prepare a charade skit from the card. Let each team present its charade for the class to guess the difficult task or situation you keep trying to solve.

## LESSON 10 PRESCHOOL GAME:
# Ball Test

**Supplies:** Two beach balls, masking tape

**Preparation:** Put two parallel lines of masking tape on the floor, each six to eight feet long. Place the lines about 18 inches apart.

**Directions:** Divide the children into two groups. Have each group sit on one of the tape lines so that the groups are facing each other. Give the beach ball to a child at the end of one line. **Each time God sent a test to Egypt, it spread through the country. Let's make our ball spread through our class.** Let the children take turns rolling the ball back and forth down the lines. You may need to name the next child in line to catch the ball to help the children know where to roll it.

When the ball has reached the end of the line, have it travel back. You may want to try playing with two balls if you have older preschoolers.

## LESSON 11 SNACK:
# Passover Snack

**Supplies:** Crackers or other unleavened bread, fresh parsley, celery leaves, beef jerky or other dried meat

**Directions:** Explain how your snack foods are similar to the lamb (beef jerky because it's meat), bitter herbs (parsley and celery leaves), and unleavened bread (crackers) that the Israelites ate. Give each child a little of each. Offer seconds when the children ask. As the children eat you might explain that at Jesus' Last Supper, Jesus gave new meaning to the Passover meal, and now we celebrate it as Communion to remind us of Christ's death and resurrection.

## LESSON 11 ELEMENTARY GAME:
# Lamb Tag

**Supplies:** None

Gather the children in a large, open area or outdoors, if suitable. Point out boundaries for the game. Ask one or two children to volunteer to be Israelites who catch lambs (the rest of the children). Tagged lambs say, "Bah, bah," as they walk out of bounds for the rest of the round.

As a variation for more challenge: Assign one child to be Moses who may attempt to save lambs from being tagged by getting in the way but who can't be tagged out by the Israelites.

## LESSON 11 PRESCHOOL GAME:
# Find the Passover Dessert

**Supplies:** Two matching cloth napkins

**Preparation:** Hide one of the cloth napkins in the area where the children will be playing.

**Directions:** Show one of the napkins to the children. **During Passover time, the father of the house hides a piece of matzo for the children to find. I have hidden a napkin that looks like this. Can you find it?** Give the children time to hunt for the napkin. When it is found, let the child who found the napkin hide it again. Continue playing as time allows.

## LESSON 12 SNACK:
# Celebration Snacks

**Supplies:** Any snack foods that children would recognize as being for a celebration (popcorn, chips and salsa, cupcakes, etc.), napkins, plates

**Directions:** Put out the celebration snack choices and let the children choose what they wish. As the children eat, ask them about foods they usually eat on happy occasions and what they like about them.

## LESSON 12 ELEMENTARY GAME:
# Red Sea Water

**Supplies:** Balloons, masking tape, watch with second hand or stopwatch

**Preparation:** Inflate balloons. Try to have two or three times as many as the number of children playing. Use masking tape to mark a very large X on the floor to make four large playing areas (one in each wedge of the X).

Divide the children into two equal groups: the Israelites and the Egyptians. Divide each group in half to form two groups of Israelites and two groups of Egyptians. Have the Israelite groups stand in opposite wedges of the X facing each other. Have the Egyptians stand in the other two wedges of the X. Spread the balloons in a circle around the X, behind the children.

Tell the children that the balloons are water in the Red Sea and they all want the water to go toward the other group. So at your signal, the two groups of Israelites will grab balloons and throw them into the playing areas of the two groups of the Egyptians. At the same time, the Egyptians will throw balloons back into the two playing areas of the Israelites. The groups may throw into either wedge of the other group.

Plan to time the children for one minute, and give the signal to begin. The children will all start grabbing balloons and throwing them at the same time. Have the Park Patrol watch to make sure children are not kicking balloons over the lines with their feet or simply scooping them in; players must pick up each balloon and toss it. When time is up, have the children stop and count the balloons that remain inside their areas. The group with the combined lowest number wins that round.

Play again as time permits.

## LESSON 12 PRESCHOOL GAME:
# Through the Sea

**Supplies:** Two blue sheets or butcher paper

**Preparation:** Lay the two sheets next to each other with a path between them. The path should go the length of the sheets and be 20 inches wide.

**Directions: Let's pretend to be the Israelites going through the Red Sea. This path is our dry land. Let's walk through the sea.** Have a Park Patrol lead the children walking through the sea. Repeat the activity with children giving suggestions on how to move through the sea—hop, skip, gallop, and so on.

# LESSON 13 SNACK:
# Snacks from Our Talents

**Supplies:** Instant pudding, milk, mixing bowl and spoon, serving bowls, spoons

**Directions:** Let the children help make instant pudding according to package directions. You might review the Bible memory verse while waiting for the pudding to set. Or let the children talk about their various talents. When ready, let everyone enjoy the benefits of their cooking talents and enjoy the pudding! For any children with allergies to dairy products, provide an alternative snack, such as pudding made with soy or rice milk.

# LESSON 13 ELEMENTARY GAME:
# Talent Races

**Supplies:** (Optional: masking tape, string)

Let the children use talents of speed and agility for Talent Races. The games will be an opportunity to reinforce that God gives us all talents.

Have the children line up in teams behind a start line. Designate an end point, and have Park Patrol members stand there to mark the spot and to see that children follow race directions. You might mark the lines with masking tape on the floor.

One teammember at a time, the children hop on one foot to the turn around point and hop on the other foot back to the start line. Anyone touching down both feet must start again. The first team to complete the relay wins that round.

Continue with other speed and agility relays, such as skipping or galloping, walking heel to toe, or walking in pairs side by side with inside legs tied together with yarn.

# LESSON 13 PRESCHOOL GAME:
# Offering Relay

**Supplies:** Baskets or paper bags, yarn, fabric, costume jewelry, yarn, and stones

**Preparation:** Put the items in the baskets or bags. You will need two bags or baskets for each type of item. Set the baskets at the far end of the area from the starting line.

**Directions:** Divide the children into two groups. Have each group form a line opposite the bags or baskets. Ask the first child in each line to hop down and get an offering of silver or gold. That child hops down, picks up the basket or bag, and hops back. Give an instruction to the second child in line, and so on, until all the children have brought an offering.

You may need to duplicate bags if you have more than five children in each line. Vary the motion the children have to make to reach the bags.

## LESSON 14 SNACK:
# God's Good Food

**Supplies:** Small cluster of grapes for each child, honey graham crackers, napkins, (optional: milk and cups)

**Directions:** Give each child some grapes and a honey graham cracker on a napkin. **How can these foods remind us of the Bible story?** (The spies brought back huge bunches of grapes, God promised it would be a land flowing with milk and honey.)

## LESSON 14 ELEMENTARY GAME:
# Going to the Promised Land

**Supplies:** None

**Directions:** This game is a variation of "Going on a Lion Hunt," which may be familiar to the children. Have the children sit in a circle. You say each phrase with the children echoing it in rhythm. They may pat their legs on the beats. Before beginning, invite the children to suggest obstacles and motions. Suggestions are included in the following rhythm. If you know the rhythm by other words or rhythm, feel free to adapt it.

**Goin' to the Promised Land!** (children echo)

**We're not scared.** (children echo)

**Got my tent in my pack** (children echo)

**And some goodies, too.** (children echo)

**Comin' to a boulder.**

**Have to get around!**

Make a motion of climbing a boulder for four beats.

Repeat the rhythm. At the underlined words, substitute any of these or use ideas from the children:

**Comin' to a river, Have to swim through** (swimming motion)

**Comin' to a mountain, Have to get over** (climbing motion)

**Comin' to <u>tall grass</u>, Have to <u>push through</u>** (sweeping with arms)

**Comin' to <u>some mud</u>, Have to <u>stomp through</u>** (stomping)

On the last verse, end with, **We're here!**

## LESSON 14 PRESCHOOL GAME:
# Spying Out the Land Relay

**Supplies:** A classroom chair, a beach towel, a basket with several pieces of play food, four or five pillows

**Preparation:** Set up four stations in a relay course like this:

1. Set a chair at the beginning as a hill.

2. Lay the beach towel on the ground as a valley.

3. Empty the basket. Lay the food around the basket.

4. Have the pillows ready to stack on top of each other to create a giant person.

**Directions:** One at a time, have the children climb over the hill, crawl through the valley, gather the food in the basket,, and carry it to the pillows. The last step is to stack the pillows to create a giant person and then run back to the group. After each child has gone back to the group, the next child can go on the relay. Repeat until each child has had a turn. You may want to have a Park Patrol empty the basket and unstack the pillows after each child.

## LESSON 15 SNACK:
# Jericho Rubble

**Supplies:** Pretzel bites, raisins, potato sticks, serving bowl and spoon, small paper plates or napkins

**Preparation:** Mix together the pretzels, raisins, and potato sticks in a serving bowl.

**Directions:** Give each child a small pile of Jericho Rubble on a plate or napkin. Tell the children to pretend this is the rubble left over after the walls of Jericho came crashing down. Let the children retell the Bible story to a Noah's Park puppet, worked by a Park Patrol helper.

## LESSON 15 ELEMENTARY GAME:
# Wall of Jericho March

**Supplies:** None

**Directions:** Have the children partner up in pairs. One will be a 1 and the other a 2 (or any designation you'd like). All the 1s will make an inner circle and the 2s will form an outer circle around them. The 1s will march in one direction and the 2s will march in the other direction. Clap out a rhythm while the children march in opposite directions.

When you call out, **"The walls of Jericho are falling!"** the partners race to find each other. When they find each other they immediately squat down. The last pair down sits off to the side and helps clap the rhythm until all are eliminated.

## LESSON 15 PRESCHOOL GAME:
# Marching around Jericho

**Supplies:** Classroom chairs

**Preparation:** Set the chairs in a circle with the seats facing in to create the city of Jericho.

**Directions:** Have the children line up behind a leader. **Let's pretend we're the army going around the city of Jericho. Let's march.** Have the leader lead the class in marching around the city. Then have the leader move to the end of the line and the next child is the new leader. **Now let's skip around Jericho.** Continue having the children taking turns leading the line in different movements around the city until each child has been a leader. Some suggested movements are hopping, galloping, walking, tiptoeing, and so on.

## LESSON 16 SNACK:
# Undercover Snacks

**Supplies:** A treat with a filling, such as cookies, granola bars, or cupcakes; napkins; drink

**Directions:** Give each child a drink and a cookie or bar. **The people of Gibeon disguised themselves by covering up their good clothes. They went "undercover" to fool Joshua and the Israelites. Our "undercover" snacks remind us of that. We don't know for sure what is in the cookies we have until we bite into them.**

## LESSON 16 ELEMENTARY GAME:
# You Can't Fool Me

**Supplies:** None

**Directions:** The children sit in a big circle. Choose one child to be IT. IT stands in the middle of the circle, slowly turning around. The children observe what IT is wearing. Then IT goes out of the room and changes one small thing in his or her appearance, such as untucking a shirt, rolling one sock up or down, removing a hair barrette or ribbon, turning a belt backward, parting hair on other side, or putting a pencil or marker in a pocket. You might want to send a Park Patrol helper out of the room with IT to help decide what to change each time. Don't make the change too hard to spot if the children are young.

IT comes back into the circle and calls on children who think they know what has changed. The child called on says, "You can't fool me. I know you changed _____." When someone guesses the change, he or she gets to be IT.

## LESSON 16 PRESCHOOL GAME:
# Tricky Tag

**Supplies:** Blindfold, Noah's Park puppet

**Directions:** Have the children sit in a wide circle on the floor or on chairs. Choose one child to be "Joshua" and blindfold him or her. Joshua stands in the middle of the circle. Choose another child to be inside the circle. That child wears the puppet. The object of the game is for the blindfolded child to catch the child holding the puppet.

Whenever Joshua calls, "Have you traveled far?" the child wearing the puppet must answer, "Ask God what to do. I might trick you." The blindfolded child moves around the circle, following the voice of the other child, who quietly tries to move away. When Joshua touches the child with the puppet, choose two other children to be in the circle.

## LESSON 17 SNACK:
# Big and Small Snacks

**Supplies:** Any cookie that comes in two sizes—a mini and a regular, or a regular and a large—or any snack that can be paired big and small, such as a raisin and an apple; napkins

**Directions:** Give each child one small snack and one big one.

Remind the children as they eat this "big and small" snack that God can help us in big or small ways.

## LESSON 17 ELEMENTARY GAME:
# The Day the Kids Stood Still

**Supplies:** Scarf or bandanna

**Directions:** You will need a large open space to play this game, or play it outside.

The children stand absolutely still until you toss the scarf into the air. When the scarf is in the air, they must giggle, howl, or laugh out loud until it hits the ground. When it touches the ground they must stop instantly and become still again. If any player breaks into a smile or giggles or howls when the scarf is on the ground, he or she is out and goes to the side. Continue until there is only one player left. Those who leave the circle can stand on the side and try to get the other players to laugh or giggle—without touching them, of course.

## LESSON 17 PRESCHOOL GAME:
# Go! The Sun Is Shining

**Supplies:** A yellow ball (or a large yellow circle of paper)

**Directions:** Have the children line up at one end of the playing area. Stand at the other end, holding the yellow ball. The ball will be the sun. When the sun is shining by being held up, the children may start moving toward it. When the sun goes down, the children have to freeze. Challenge the children to freeze quickly when the sun goes down. Repeat holding up the sun and lowering it until all the children reach you.

Play several times to encourage the children to understand the relationship of cause (because the sun is shining) and effect (they can move).

## LESSON 18 SNACK:
# Good Chocolate Chip Cookies

**Supplies:** Really good chocolate chip cookies, napkins

**Directions: For our class this morning I made some terrible chocolate chip cookies that no one, including me, wanted to eat. Why were they terrible? Because I didn't follow the directions! In today's lesson we learned that it is important to pay attention to God's directions. The person who made these good cookies *followed* the directions. As you enjoy these *good* cookies, let's remember today's Bible story.**

Give each child one or two cookies, and let them eat as they share about experiences they've had helping in the kitchen.

## LESSON 18 ELEMENTARY GAME:
# Samuel Says

**Supplies:** None

**Directions:** This game is similar to "Simon Says." Have the children spread out in an uncluttered area.

Choose one player to begin as Samuel. Samuel's job is to call out, "Samuel says _____ (describe an action such as, jumping, turn around, touch your toes, burp, laugh out loud, etc.)" while demonstrating the action the group should mimic.

Everyone in the group must do what Samuel says *only* if he begins his command with the phrase "Samuel says." If Samuel describes and demonstrates an action but doesn't say, "Samuel says," the group should ignore the command. If anyone does the action anyway, he or she must leave the group until the next round. The last one standing is the winner and gets to be Samuel next.

## LESSON 18 PRESCHOOL GAME:
# Calling Game

**Supplies:** Bath or beach towels (from the Preschool Bible Story)

**Preparation:** Fold each towel in half. Make a line of towels across one end of your playing area.

**Directions:** The children sit on the towels. Tell the children that you are Eli. Stand at the area opposite the towels. **Samuel thought Eli was calling him. Listen carefully to what Eli says.** Call out something like, **"Samuel! Samuel! Hop to me."** The children stand up and hop to where you are standing. When all the children have reached you, send them back to "bed."

Continue playing, changing the action each time. Some possible actions are skipping, walking, taking baby steps, and so on.

## LESSON 19 SNACK:
# Choices

**Supplies:** A variety of snacks on a tray, such as cookies, veggies, or chips; paper plates; napkins

**Directions: Today we have been talking about making good choices. Our snack is made up of several things. You can choose just one. Many times choosing one thing means *not* choosing another thing. That is what makes choices so hard.** As children eat, let them talk about whether their snack choice was hard for them or not.

## LESSON 19 ELEMENTARY GAME:
# The King Wants to Know

**Supplies:** Chairs

**Directions:** Place chairs in a circle for each child except one. Choose one child to be the king. He or she stands in the middle with eyes closed while turning around, pointing and saying:

*"The north wind blows*

*"And the king wants to know."*

On the word "know," he opens his eyes and the child he has pointed to must answer his question. The questions are easy ones such as: *"What is your favorite food? What is your favorite color? Do you have a pet?"* The child answers and then says:

*"What else does the king want to know?"*

Then the king asks a general category question such as:

*"The king wants to know who likes pizza"* or *"Who has blue eyes?"*

Everyone who fits that category must jump up and find another seat while the kings tries to take a seat. Whoever is left standing becomes the king.

You will need to help the children with appropriate questions and remembering the steps of this game until they get used to it.

## LESSON 19 PRESCHOOL GAME:
# Donkeys or a Crown?

**Supplies:** 12 two-inch circles of paper, pen, Noah's Park puppet

**Preparation:** Draw a donkey on 11 of the circles. Draw a crown on the last circle. Hide the circles around the room.

**Directions:** Explain to the children that paper circles are hidden in the room. **Some have donkeys on them, like the ones Saul lost. One has a crown on it because God chose Saul to be the king.**

Give the children time to look for the circles. Use a Noah's Park puppet to give clues to any children who need help.

Hide the circles again to continue the game.

## LESSON 20 SNACK:
# Power Snacks

**Supplies:** A healthy energy bar or raisins and fruit slices, napkins

**Preparation:** If the energy bars are big, you may want to cut them in half.

**Directions: Today's story was about God's power and how it is bigger than our biggest problem. This snack is full of power too. It will give us energy, just as God's power gave David strength and energy to fight Goliath.** Let the Park Patrol help pass out the snack to the children.

## LESSON 20: ELEMENTARY GAME
# What Time Is It, Goliath?

**Supplies:** None

**Directions:** This game is best played in a large, open area.

Select one child to start as Goliath. Goliath stands with his or her back to the children. The rest of the children stand about 20 yards back, at a start line. The children call out: "What time is it, Goliath?"

Goliath answers in a big, booming voice, "It is ___ o'clock." Goliath picks a time, such as four o'clock. The children take that many steps (such as four) toward Goliath.

Again the children ask, "What time is it, Goliath?" And again, Goliath answers with a different time, and the children proceed toward him or her that number of steps.

Continue in this fashion until Goliath thinks the children are getting close. Then he or she may answer, "It's dinner time!" and turns to chase the children back to the start line. When Goliath touches one of the children, that child becomes the new Goliath and the game starts over.

## LESSON 20 PRESCHOOL GAME:
# What Should I Take to Fight?

**Supplies:** Paper circles

**Preparation:** Draw a stone, a sword, or a shield on each of the paper circles.

**Directions: David fought with a stone.** Show a circle with a stone on it. **Goliath fought with a sword and a shield.** Show those pictures to the children.

Have the children sit in a circle in chairs or on the floor. Give each child a paper circle to hold. Call one of the pictures. The children holding the circles with that picture jump up and walk or run to switch places. Call out another picture, and let those children run to switch places too. Continue to call out pictures and let the children exchange seats. If you have younger preschoolers, hold up a circle to help the children recognize it.

After a few minutes, invite the children to switch circles with someone sitting next to them so that all the children end up with a different picture. Then continue playing.

## LESSON 21 SNACK:
# Thankful-Heart Sandwiches

**Supplies:** Bread, sunflower seed butter, jelly, heart-shaped cookie cutter, paper plates, napkins, water or juice and cups.

**Preparation:** Make sunflower seed butter and jelly sandwiches. (If there are no children or visitors with nut allergies in your class, you may use peanut butter.) Cut heart shapes from the sandwiches.

**Today we learned that we should have thankful hearts instead of being jealous. Our snack reminds us of that. Let's thank God for this snack and for all the people who help make Children's Church fun.**

After a brief prayer, give each child a sandwich heart to enjoy.

## LESSON 21 ELEMENTARY GAME:
# Cat and Mouse

**Supplies:** A stuffed or toy mouse and cat

**Directions:** Have the children sit in a circle, on the floor or on chairs.

**In today's Bible story, Saul was always trying to get David, like a cat chasing a mouse. That is the game we are playing today, "Cat and Mouse."**

Start a mouse around the circle, passing it from child to child. When mouse is halfway around the circle, start the cat around. The cat can change directions and is trying to catch the mouse. The mouse can change directions too and should always try to stay opposite cat. The children playing choose when to send an animal in the other direction. When mouse is caught, the game starts over.

# LESSON 21 PRESCHOOL GAME:
# Happy/Sad Game

**Supplies:** One happy/sad face puppet from the Preschool Bible Story

**Directions:** Have the children stand at the end of the room opposite from you. **Let's play a game with our happy and sad face puppet. When I hold up the happy face, you may take one step forward. When I hold up the sad face, stand still.**

Play the game by holding up the different faces of the puppet. Since all the children are moving at the same rate, they should all reach the leader at the same time.

To play again, suggest the children take giant steps or baby steps.

## LESSON 22 SNACK:
# Friendship Snack

**Supplies:** Two or three snacks of your choice—cookies, crackers, popcorn, fruit—in resealable plastic baggies (two baggies for each child)

**Preparation:** Place a handful of each snack in its own baggie.

**Directions:** Let the children choose two snacks each, but tell them not to start eating until you give the signal. Then tell them to give the best snack—their favorite—to someone else in the class.

Make sure no one gets two "best" snacks and that no one is left out from getting a favorite. You might want to have the children give their "gift" snack to their memory verse partner or to the person on their right.

**Today we learned that the best kind of friend is an unselfish friend. By sharing our best snack with someone else, we are being unselfish friends.**

## LESSON 22 ELEMENTARY GAME:
# Smiles, Handshakes, or Hugs

**Supplies:** None

**Directions:** This game is a variation of "Rock, Paper, Scissors." Have the children stand up in an open area.

**We are going to greet each other in three different ways.**

**One: a smile.** Hold up one finger.

**Two: a high five.** Hold up two fingers.

**Three: a hug.** Hold up three fingers.

**When I give the signal, walk up to someone and together you will count, "one, two, three," while hitting your fist on the palm of your other hand—like the game "Rock, Paper, Scissors." On "three" you will each display one, two, or three fingers on your hand. If you both show three fingers,**

you hug each other. If you both show two fingers, you give a high five. If you both show one finger, you both smile and say, "Hi." If the number of your fingers is different, you do the action of the lowest number. For example, if one of you shows three fingers and one of you shows only one, you both smile and say, "Hi." After you play this game once, you move on to someone else and repeat it all again.

Demonstrate the game with the Park Patrol so that everyone understands. The children will enjoy playing the game with the Park Patrol helpers and other leaders in the group. If it is a small class, they may be able to greet everyone in the room.

## LESSON 22 PRESCHOOL GAME:
# Elbow to Elbow—Friend to Friend

**Supplies:** None

**Directions: A best friend is an unselfish friend. David and Jonathan were best friends. Let's play a game with our friends.**

Divide the children into groups of two, using a Park Patrol helper if you have an odd number.

When you call out, "Elbow to elbow," the friends should put their elbows together. Use other body parts that preschoolers can easily identify to put together, such as back, foot, hand, ear, knee, and shoulder. When you say, "Friend to friend," the pairs can choose any two body parts—even if they don't match.

## LESSON 23 SNACK:
# A Snack for David's Army

**Supplies:** Pita bread (pocket bread), sunflower seed butter or cream cheese, jelly, plastic knives, disposable plates, napkins, cups of water

**Preparation:** Cut each pita bread circle into fourths.

**Directions:** Give each child one triangle of pita bread on a plate and a cup of water. Place the other things so the children can reach them. Let the children spread sunflower seed butter or cream cheese inside the pocket of their bread. Have Park Patrol help them, if needed.

As the children eat, explain that David's army was in hiding and probably had only bread, similar to pita bread, and water.

## LESSON 23 ELEMENTARY GAME:
# Finding Saul's Spear

**Supplies:** Spear and water jug from the Elementary Bible Story

**Directions:** Pick someone to begin as David. David leaves the room while the group decides on a hiding place for the spear and jug. Call David back in. The group says to David, "Can you find Saul's spear and jug?" As David begins to look, the group gives him or her clues by pretending to be warm, then hot, while David is getting closer to the hiding place. The group pretends to get cold and shiver when David moves away from the hiding place. When Saul's things are found, another David is chosen. If the spear and jug are too big to hide in the classroom, you can use something smaller to represent them.

# LESSON 23 PRESCHOOL GAME:
# Tag a King

**Supplies:** None

**Directions:** Have the children spread out in your game area. Choose one child to begin as IT. This child tries to tag the other children, while they try to avoid being touched. Whenever someone is tagged, that child has to call out, "God's way is best." Then this child becomes the new IT and tries to tag others.

## LESSON 24 SNACK:
# Lemonade and Donuts

**Supplies:** Lemonade, small donuts, disposable cups, plates or napkins

**Directions: This morning we heard about the tough life of a lemon. Think about a donut—he has a tough life too, being poked and fried. Let's thank God for these good snacks that have tough lives so that we can enjoy them!**

Lead the children in a prayer of thanks. Then Let the Park Patrol pass out donuts on a napkin or plate and a cup of lemonade to each child.

## LESSON 24 ELEMENTARY GAME:
# David and the Amalekites

**Supplies:** Something to mark sidelines and end lines

**Directions:** This game is best played outdoors or in a large indoor area, like a gym. Choose someone to be David. He or she stands in the middle of the field and can run anywhere inbounds but can't cross an end line. All the "Amalekites" line up behind one of the end lines. At a signal, the Amalekites dash through the field, being careful not to run outside the boundaries. If David tags them, they become part of David's army and chase Amalekites too. If they are not tagged and can get to the other end line, they are safe and wait for the next signal to cross again. When the last Amalekite is caught, he or she becomes the new David, and the game starts over.

## LESSON 24 PRESCHOOL GAME:
# Can You Help Me Find My Brother (or Sister)?

**Supplies:** Noah's Park Puppet

**Directions:** Have the children sit in a circle. Choose one child to wear the puppet and stand in the center. Begin the game with: **David and his men were looking for their families. Let's play a game where we pretend we are each other's brothers and sisters.** (Puppet's name)**, can you help me find my brother** (or sister)**? He has . . .**" Give a couple of details about one of the children in the circle. Add details about that child until the "puppet" (the child in the middle) identifies the child being described. That child becomes the next one to wear the puppet.

Continue playing until each child has had a turn being a brother or sister.

## LESSON 25 SNACK:
# Celebration Cookies

**Supplies:** Oatmeal raisin cookies or any cookie with raisins or dates, napkins

**Directions: In our Bible story we learned about the celebration that David planned. He gave out cakes with dates and raisins to all the people. These oatmeal raisin cookies will remind us of David's celebration.**

Give each child one or two cookies on a napkin. Be aware of any food allergies that some children may have and provide an alternate snack for them. As the children eat, you might discuss common foods of Bible times, such as dates and raisins.

## LESSON 25 ELEMENTARY GAME:
# David's Celebration Dance

**Supplies:** CD player and Noah's Park CD

**Directions:** Have the children scatter around the room in a large playing area. Choose one child to begin as IT, and he or she leaves the room. Then choose someone to be David. When the music starts, David begins a dance movement that the others imitate. The rest of the players should immediately begin the same movement. IT returns to the room and tries to guess who is being David and leading the dance motions. David keeps changing the movement when IT is not looking. The other players should only glance toward David briefly so as not to give away his or her identity. Caution the child playing David to not change movements frequently and confuse the other players. When IT guesses who is leading the dancing, he or she gets to be David, and the game begins again with a new IT.

## LESSON 25 PRESCHOOL GAME:
# The King's Parade

**Supplies:** Noah's Park puppet, Noah's Park CD, CD player

**Directions:** Invite the children to join you in a parade as God's ark is brought into David's city. Have the children line up in single file. Play songs from the Noah's Park CD for the children to move to. Give a puppet to the first child in line. That child chooses an action for everyone to do as he or she leads the parade. This child can march, tiptoe, slide, sway, walk backward, sidestep, and so on. After half a minute, pause the parade and give the puppet to the next child in line. The previous leader goes to the end of the line. Play long enough for every child to have a chance to be a leader.

## LESSON 26 SNACK:
# ABCs of Wisdom

**Supplies:** Alphabet letter cereal, disposable plates

**Directions:** Have the children sit in small groups. Pour some alphabet cereal on a central plate for each group. One at a time, each child takes a letter from the plate and names something wise they could ask God for that begins with the letter. For example, if a child picked up the letter O, he or she could say, "Obey my parents." After naming something, the child may eat the letter.

Continue twice around each circle. Then give each child a plate, pour on some cereal, and let the children enjoy eating their snack a little faster!

## LESSON 26 ELEMENTARY GAME:
# What Would I Want?

**Supplies:** None

**Directions:** Have the children sit in a large circle. The children need to think of what they would wish to receive if they were asked, "What would you like to get if you could have anything?"

Choose a child to stand in the center. Ask a child sitting in the circle to tell the group his or her wish. (Encourage all the children to answer in just a word or two, such as "a puppy.") The child in the center repeats the wish. Then let the next seated child give his or her response. The child in the center points to the first child and names that answer and then points the second child and tells that answer. Continue on to the third child and have the center child now name all three responses in order. Keep doing this until the child in the center makes a mistake or makes it all the way around the circle. Choose a new person to go into the center and the children think of a new wish.

## LESSON 26 PRESCHOOL GAME:
# Follow the King

**Supplies:** A paper crown

**Directions: Solomon asked God for wisdom. Our King Solomon will know the right things to do as we follow him.** Let a Park Patrol helper begin as King Solomon (wearing the crown), and have all the children line up behind him or her. King Solomon leads the children around obstacles, out and back in the classroom door, under tables, and so on. The leader should also add arm movements, such as flapping or clapping, and ways to walk, such as hopping or walking backward. Choose different children to be King Solomon if you have time.

## LESSON 27 SNACK:
# Where's My Snack?

**Supplies:** Any fruit or raw vegetable with dip, tray, two bowls

Cut out one side of a large box. Set the fruit, tray, and bowls inside the box. Have a Park Patrol helper turn the bowls upside down on the tray and then put a snack (several pieces of fruit or vegetables) under one bowl. Then put the tray on top of the box and have a child come and make a "wise choice" to pick which bowl has the snack. If the child chooses correctly, he can have the snack. If not, he sits back down and waits to have another turn. The Park Patrol helpers then set up the snack for the next child to choose. Continue until all children have a snack.

Set a bowl of dip on the table where the children will eat once they have their snack. Children may use a spoon to scoop some of the dip onto their plates. If you have a large group or are short on time, set up more than one hiding box.

## LESSON 27 ELEMENTARY GAME:
# Who Did It?

**Supplies:** Blindfold, baby doll from the Elementary Bible Story or any smaller object

Have the children stand in a large circle in an area with a lot of space. Choose a child to begin as "Solomon" and stand in the middle of the circle. Place an object on the ground behind Solomon and put the blindfold on Solomon. Have the circle of children walk clockwise around Solomon. Point to a child, who quietly sneaks up and takes the object. After the child returns to the circle, have the children stop walking and stand facing Solomon with their hands behind their backs, pretending to hold the object. Take the blindfold off Solomon. He or she makes three guesses to try to determine which child took the object. If guessed "wisely," that child remains as Solomon. But if all three guesses are inaccurate, the child who took the object becomes the new Solomon. Continue playing until all children have been able to play the role of Solomon.

## LESSON 27 PRESCHOOL GAME:
# King Solomon, May I?

**Supplies:** Wisdom Scepter (from the Preschool Bible Story)

**Directions:** Choose one child to be King Solomon and hold the scepter. Have the king stand at one end of the room. The other children should line up at the opposite end of the room.

The king calls out different commands, such as, "Take three giant steps." The children need to respond, "King Solomon, may I?" before they can move the stated number of steps. If a child moves without asking the question, he or she returns to the starting point. The first child to reach King Solomon becomes the new king.

## LESSON 28 SNACK:
# Build a Snack

**Supplies:** Marshmallows (large and small), grapes, cheese cut into sticks or blocks, crackers of all sizes and shapes, paper plates, napkins, (optional: sunflower seed spread, marshmallow spread)

Today's lesson about Solomon's building a temple for God can inspire the children to use the snack items to build something. Let the kids play around and build structures—much smaller than Solomon's temple! Set out a variety of items on a platter and let the children choose some to put on their plate and build with. If you'd like, provide "glue" in the form of sunflower seed butter or marshmallow crème.

## LESSON 28 ELEMENTARY GAME:
# Temple Workers Mix-up

**Supplies:** Classroom chairs

**Directions:** Divide the children into four groups. Give each group a name of one of the workers from the temple: wood-carvers, stone-cutters, woodcutters, gold decorators. Put chairs in a big circle, but have one fewer chair than the number of children.

Have the children sit in the chairs, but mix up so they aren't next to members of their group. Choose one child to be in the center. The child in the center calls out one or more group names. The members of that group quickly change places with someone else. The child in the center is also trying to grab one of the empty seats. The child without a seat stays in the center and is the next to call a group. Continue playing to allow most children the opportunity to be in the center.

## LESSON 28 PRESCHOOL GAME:
# Building the Temple

**Supplies:** Large cardboard blocks or blocks made from paper lunch bags (three to four blocks for each child)

**Preparation:** If making blocks, stuff paper bags with newspapers and tape them shut in a box shape.

**Directions:** Put the blocks on one side of the playing area. Have the children line up behind the blocks. A Park Patrol helper can be King Solomon standing at the other end of the playing area. Designate a temple area by Solomon.

One at a time, have a child run a block to King Solomon and place it somewhere on the temple area. The next child can bring a block when the first child comes back. Continue with the children taking turns until all the blocks have been used. The shape of the temple doesn't matter, and the children may stack the blocks or simply set them on the floor.

## LESSON 29 SNACK:
# Be Wise Snack

**Supplies:** Graham crackers, chocolate syrup in a squeezable bottle, paper plates, napkins

**Directions:** Give each child a graham cracker on a plate and instruct the children not to break it into sections yet. Take the bottle of syrup to each child and let him or her squeeze the bottle to write the words "Be wise" on a graham cracker. Ask Park Patrol members to help younger children.

You may want to print "Be wise" on the board for children to copy. If you have a large group, supply two or more bottles of chocolate syrup. If some letters are smeared, encourage the children not to worry about it but to simply enjoy eating the crackers!

## LESSON 29 ELEMENTARY GAME:
# Come, Be Wise

**Supplies:** None

**Directions:** This game is similar to "Red Light, Green Light" but substitute the words "Not wise" for "red light" and "Be wise" for "green light." Choose one child to stand at the opposite end of the room facing away from the group and be the caller. This child will call out "Not wise" or "Be wise." The group can run forward when the child calls, "Be wise," but must stop when they hear the words, "Not wise." The caller quickly turns around to see if any children are still moving after calling, "Not wise." Any kids caught moving go back to the start line. The first person to touch the caller becomes the new caller. Play several rounds so that different children get the opportunity to become the caller.

## PRESCHOOL GAME
# Jeroboam Tag

**Supplies:** None

**Directions:** You or a Park Patrol helper will be IT. IT tries to tag the children. When a child has been tagged, IT says, "Come to *my* kingdom." The tagged child joins hands with IT. They continue holding hands and tagging children until all the children have been caught and the entire class is holding hands.

## LESSON 30 SNACK:
# Apple Consequence Snack

**Supplies:** Apple and applesauce, bowls, cinnamon, plastic spoons

Hold up an apple and ask what the consequence would be if you crushed the apple. (Applesauce, apple juice, etc.) Have the Park Patrol helpers scoop the applesauce into the bowls. Some children might like to sprinkle cinnamon on their applesauce.

## LESSON 30 ELEMENTARY GAME:
# What's My Consequence?

**Supplies:** None

**Directions:** This game is similar to "Simon Says" but with consequences. Have the children stand and spread out in the room, facing you. As you give various fun commands, the children must listen carefully for the words, "Simon Says." When you say, "Simon says," before a command, the kids should follow the command. If you say the command without first saying "Simon says," the children should stand still.

The children don't have to sit out if they make a mistake. Instead, give them a consequence, such as doing five jumping jacks, saying the memory verse, and so on.

Suggested commands for Simon Says: take a big step sideways, clap your hands three times, shake someone's hand, say your full name and address.

# LESSON 30 PRESCHOOL GAME:
# Shelter-by-the-Brook Relay

**Supplies:** Masking tape, two baskets, two pieces of crumpled paper for each child

**Preparation:** Put two lines of masking tape six inches apart at the far end of your playing area. This will be the brook. Set the baskets on the other side of the brook. Crumple up paper so that each child will have two pieces.

**Directions: Let's pretend that we are the birds who brought meat and bread to Elijah.** Ask a Park Patrol helper to sit between the baskets as "Elijah." Divide the children into two groups. Line up the groups at the end of the area opposite the brook. The first child should pick up a crumpled piece of paper, hop to the brook, jump over the brook, put the paper in the basket, and then run back to the end of the line. Every child should go through the exercise one time. Repeat a second time with each child skipping to the brook.

## LESSON 31 SNACK:
# Elijah's Drought Food

**Supplies:** Banana bread or other kinds of fruit breads, napkins, cups of water

Let each child have a cup of water and a slice of bread. As the children eat, discuss how Elijah ate bread (though not as fancy) and water during the drought. Let a Noah's Park puppet visit the children and ask what they like to eat when they're really, really hungry.

## LESSON 31 ELEMENTARY GAME:
# Elijah's Bread and Water

**Supplies:** Plastic toy bread (or real slices of bread), cups half-filled with water, (optional: 8" x 11" cardboard, towels for cleanup)

**Directions:** This game is best played outdoors. Line up the children in teams for a relay. Give each team a piece of toy bread (or a slice of real bread). As an option, you could have each team use a piece of cardboard. The first player on each team balances the bread on his or her head. At your signal, those players run to an end point and back without letting the bread fall and without touching it. Then they give the bread to the next player on their team. See which teams can successfully carry the bread back and forth. You don't have to make this a race.

If playing outdoors or in an area where some water spills are okay, play a second round, this time with players carrying a cup half full of water. The goal is to reach the end and back without spilling the water.

## LESSON 31 PRESCHOOL GAME:
# Baking Bread

**Supplies:** Twin or full flat sheet (or a small parachute)

**Directions:** Spread the sheet on the floor. Space the children equally around the edges. Have the children bend down, grip the edge of the sheet with both hands, and stand up straight.

**God sent Elijah to a woman. She made bread with the oil and flour she had left. She shared the bread with Elijah.** Ask the children to lay the sheet flat on the floor. Then have them lift up the sheet over their heads as high as possible. Then have all the children quickly kneel down, bringing the edges of the sheet to the floor. This will trap air inside the sheet, creating a "loaf of bread."

**God provided enough oil and flour to make a loaf of bread the next day.** Have the children make another loaf of bread.

**And God provided enough oil and flour to make a loaf of bread the next day.** Have the children make another loaf of bread.

**And God provided enough oil and flour to make a loaf of bread the next day.** Have the children make another loaf of bread.

**And God provided enough oil and flour to make a loaf of bread every day until it rained.** Have the children make another loaf of bread.

## LESSON 32 SNACK:
# Prayer Pretzels

**Supplies:** Pretzels in their traditional shape, napkins, cups of water

**Directions:** Give each child a few pretzels on a napkin and a cup of water. As the children eat, tell them about the history of the pretzel:

**It is believed that a monk thousands of years ago invented the pretzel by rolling bread dough into the shape we know. The part of the pretzel that crosses shows hands folded in prayer. The three holes in the pretzel remind us of the three parts of God—Father, Son, and Holy Spirit.**

## LESSON 32 ELEMENTARY GAME:
# Answer Me

**Supplies:** Blindfold, cones or chairs to mark game boundaries

**Directions:** If the weather is good and you have a large open space outdoors, take the children outside to play this game. Mark off boundaries for the game with cones or chairs.

Choose one child to be blindfolded. The rest of the children scatter around inside the boundaries. The children have to remain still as a statue, unless they call out, "Can you hear me?" When they call out, they can take three steps in any direction. The blindfolded child can move freely around and tries to tag the other children. If a child is tagged, he or she steps outside of the boundaries and waits for a new game. Play continues until one child remains untagged. The untagged child gets to become the child that is blindfolded. Start another new game with all the children playing.

## LESSON 32 PRESCHOOL GAME:
# Listen to the Whisper

**Supplies:** None

**Directions:** Tell the children that God listens to our prayers, even when we whisper or pray them silently in our heads. Divide the children into teams of four or five and have them line up. Then have the last child in each line stay put while the others take a few giant steps apart from one another to spread out.

Whisper a short sentence to the first player on each team. Use sentences such as "Jesus loves you," "God listens when we pray," and "I love coming to Children's Church." At your signal, the children you whispered to run to the next player on their team and whisper the same phrase. Then that child runs to the next player and whispers what he or she heard. Continue down the line until the last child on each team has heard the whispered sentence. When everyone is finished, let all the last players tell what they heard. Repeat the game with other sentences.

## LESSON 33 SNACK:
# Big "G" Snacks

**Supplies:** Choice of little snacks: fish crackers, cereal, raisins, jelly beans, etc.; paper plates

Let Park Patrol helpers put a small scoopful or handful of snack items on each plate. Have the kids arrange their snack to form an uppercase G. Remind the children that Elijah and the Israelites chose to follow the one and only God. You may want to hold up the sign "God" from the story time. Before they eat their snack, let each child affirm that he or she will follow God.

## LESSON 33 ELEMENTARY GAME
# Follow Me

**Supplies:** None

Elijah and the Israelites chose to follow God. Lead the children in a game of "Follow the Leader." If you are able to be outdoors, let the kids do actions like rolling in the grass, kicking a ball, somersaults, cartwheels, and so on. Some indoor actions could be hopping, skipping, walking sideways, tiptoeing, giant steps, and so on. Stop periodically and choose a different child to take over the role of leader.

## LESSON 33 PRESCHOOL GAME:
# Building-Block Altar

**Supplies:** Large cardboard blocks or blocks made from lunch–size bags (three to four per child), pieces of crumpled tissue paper

**Preparation:** If using paper bags, stuff them with newspapers and tape them shut in a box shape.

**Directions:** Have the children work together to create an altar like the one Elijah built. Ask the children to take turns bringing and placing blocks for the altar. When the altar is finished, have the children shout, "There is only one God!" Have them place the "flames" of tissue paper on the altar.

If you have a large group of preschoolers, divide the children into two groups. Have a Park Patrol helper work with one of the groups.

## LESSON 34 SNACK:
# Comfort Food

**Supplies:** Bread, a variety of spreads for bread (jelly, sunflower seed butter, cinnamon, chocolate hazelnut spread, etc.), paper plates, napkins

**God sent an angel to comfort Elijah by bringing him bread and water. Let's "comfort" each other by preparing snacks for a friend.**

Have the kids get in pairs. Let each child ask their partner what they want on their bread. Each child will prepare a snack to "comfort" their friend.

## LESSON 34 ELEMENTARY GAME:
# Who Cared for Me?

**Supplies:** Plastic cup, paper plate with a piece of bread on it

Choose a child to be Elijah. Have the rest of the children gather in a circle around Elijah. When you give the signal, Elijah will lie down and sleep. The rest of the children quietly walk around him or her in a circle. Hand the cup and bread to one of the children. Have the group bring the circle in closer to Elijah while the child quietly sneaks up and places the food down by Elijah. The child should shake Elijah and then all of the kids run back and sit on the floor.

Elijah may open his or her eyes when shaken and tries to guess which child cared for him or her with the food. If the child chooses correctly, the child who brought the food becomes the new Elijah. If Elijah guesses incorrectly, choose a new child to be Elijah. Keep playing for as long as you have time.

## LESSON 34 PRESCHOOL GAME:
# Where Is God?

**Supplies:** Three pieces of paper labeled: W (wind), E (earthquake), and F (fire); tape

**Preparation:** Tape each piece of paper in a different area of the room.

**Directions:** Gather the children in the center of the room. **Different things passed by Elijah while he was waiting for God to pass by. There was a big, strong wind.** Point to the "W" paper. **There was an earthquake.** Point to the paper with the "E" on it. **And there was a fire.** Point to the paper with the "F" on it.

**Skip to see if God is in the big, strong wind.** The children should skip to the "W" paper and back. **Hop to see if God is in the earthquake.** The children should hop to the "E" paper and back. **Run to see if God is in the fire.** The children should run to the "F" paper and back.

Continue the game with the children suggesting different actions.

## LESSON 35 SNACK:
# Disappearing Snack

**Supplies:** Graham crackers, white frosting, (optional: blue food coloring)

**Preparation:** As an option, you may add blue food coloring to white frosting so that it more clearly represents the Jordan River.

**Directions:** Have the children take a block of graham cracker without breaking it into smaller bricks and spread frosting across it. Remind the children to leave the center dry so that Elisha and Elijah can cross. Before eating, the children break the cracker in half to show that Elijah and Elisha walked across the middle on dry ground. Then they can make the cracker "disappear" (by eating it) just as Elijah disappeared in the whirlwind.

## LESSON 35 ELEMENTARY GAME:
# Two-Kid Tag

**Supplies:** Two coats, obstacles (tables, chairs, wastebaskets, empty boxes, or appropriate classroom items)

**Preparation:** Set up a short, simple obstacle course. (You may let the Park Patrol help you.) You could set up tables to crawl under, chairs to climb over, wastebaskets to circle around, boxes or blocks to zigzag between, and so on.

**Directions:** Have all the children pair up. Let a Park Patrol member play if you have an uneven number of children. The first pair begins by picking up a coat and putting it on, with each partner having one arm in a sleeve. Then they quickly go through the obstacle course. When they complete the course, they holler, "Learn from people who follow God," take off the coat and hand it to the next pair waiting. Let a second pair begin the course when the first pair is about halfway through, so that you have two pairs doing the course at once.

## LESSON 35 PRESCHOOL GAME:
# Coat Tag

**Supplies:** A towel

**Directions:** Choose one child to be IT and carry the towel (Elijah's coat). Explain to the class that IT is looking for people who follow God. IT will run around unit he or she tags someone. When tagged, IT needs to place the towel (coat) around that child's shoulders. Then that child becomes the new IT.

## LESSON 36 SNACK:
# Guess How Many

**Supplies:** Small-size snack (cereal pieces, fish crackers, raisins, small candies, etc.), disposable bowls or cups, napkins

**Preparation:** Place a slightly different number of snack pieces in each bowl or cup.

Have the children take a small bowl or cup full of snack with a napkin and sit with a friend. Explain that just as Daniel had to solve problems, the kids are going to solve the problem of how many snack pieces are in their bowl. Each child looks into the other's bowl and makes a guess of how many are there. There each child counts out their snack pieces on a napkin. Have the children congratulate each other on guessing close. Then the children may enjoy their snacks.

## LESSON 36 ELEMENTARY GAME:
# In-the-Dark Walk

**Supplies:** Classroom objects for a simple obstacle course, (optional: black garbage bags, flashlight, blindfolds)

**Preparation:** Plan to completely darken you room or use a room that can be darkened. You might tape black garbage bags over the windows. If you don't have a room that can be completely darkened, have the children wear blindfolds. Set up a simple obstacle course using classroom tables and chairs.

**King Nebuchadnezzar was asleep at night—in the dark— when he had his dream. He didn't know what it meant and was "in the dark"! To be "in the dark" can mean that we don't understand or don't know what to do. When we have a problem, sometimes we feel "in the dark"! Let's walk "in the dark" to remind us that God always knows what to do and where to lead us.**

Have the children line up and hold hands. (If using blindfolds, help the kids put them on.) Then darken the room. Hold the hand of the first child in line, and use a flashlight to lead the children through the obstacle course. Continually reassure them that even though they are in the dark, you are leading them safely. If time permits, let the children change spots in line and lead them through the course again.

## LESSON 36 PRESCHOOL GAME:
# Crown Freeze Tag

**Supplies:** Crown

**Directions:** Choose one child to begin as Nebuchadnezzar and wear the crown. The other children scatter around him or her. Nebuchadnezzar tries to tag other children, but he or she can only take giant steps—no running. The other children may only tiptoe away from the king.

Whenever Nebuchadnezzar tags someone, that child must kneel down (praying to God for help) until "unfrozen" by being touched by another child. Play for about minute; then switch who gets to be Nebuchadnezzar. Continue to play and switch for the time you have allotted.

## LESSON 37 SNACK:
# Fiery Snack Scene

**Supplies:** Shredded marble cheese (yellow, orange, and white), marshmallows or another snack that stands up

Let the children arrange their shredded cheese to be like the fire in the furnace. Remind the children that when King Nebuchadnezzar looked into the furnace, he saw four men walking. The fourth man could have been an angel or even Jesus. Give each child four marshmallows to represent Shadrach, Meshach, Abenego, and the angel. Children may arrange the scene before eating it.

## LESSON 37 ELEMENTARY GAME:
# Following God through the Noise

**Supplies:** Rhythm instruments, blindfold

Choose three children to begin as the three friends from the Bible story—Shadrach, Meshach, and Abednego. Give all the other children rhythm instruments and have them spread out in the game area. Blindfold one of the three friends. Hide a Bible somewhere in the game area.

At your signal, the children all start playing their instruments, making as much noise as they can. At the same time, the two friends who aren't blindfolded start giving directions to the blindfolded friend to guide him or her through the children and over to the Bible. They may not touch the blindfolded friend, only speak to him or her. The blindfolded friend will have to trust their instructions to find the Bible. The children playing instruments should not move; the blindfolded child must be guided around them. Once the Bible is reached, choose three more children to be the three friends, hide the Bible in a new spot, and play again.

## LESSON 37 PRESCHOOL GAME:
# Touch the King

**Supplies:** Rhythm instrument

Today's game is a version of "Red Light, Green Light." Choose a child to be King Nebuchadnezzar and hold the rhythm instrument. The rest of the children line up at the opposite end of the playing area. When King Nebuchadnezzar turns his or her back to the group, the children quietly sneak toward the front. As soon as the king sounds the instrument, all of the children must instantly stop and drop to their knees. The king turns around and if he or she catches any child still moving, the child goes back to the starting line. When the king turns around again, the children can begin advancing. The first child to touch the king becomes king for the next game.

## LESSON 38 SNACK:
# Finger Writing

**Supplies:** Baby carrots, dip (ranch dressing, sour cream dip, etc.), paper plates, napkins, (optional: food coloring)

**Preparation:** If using ranch dressing, add food color so it shows up on white plates.

Give each child a plate with some carrots and dip. Let the children use a carrot like a finger to scoop some dip and write their name on the plate. See if they can read the "message" on each other's plates.

## LESSON 38 ELEMENTARY GAME:
# Secret Message Relay

**Supplies:** None

**Directions:** Divide the class into two teams. Have half of each team go to the other side of the room while the other half of each team stays near you. Have each group of children form a line. Choose a child from each team near you to come to you. Read a message to them. They will run to the other side of the room and whisper it to a child on their team. That child runs to the group on the near side of the room and whispers it to a child on their team. The children relay the message back and forth until all team members have heard the message. The last team member to hear the message runs to you and says the message. If the message is correct, the team wins. If not, retell the message. Play continues until one team gets the message correct.

**Possible messages:** *God sends the answers you need. God gives courage to do what's right. God helps you solve any problem. Learn from people who follow God. Choose to follow God. A nation that disobeys God is in trouble.*

# LESSON 38 PRESCHOOL GAME:
# Party Relay

**Supplies:** Two party hats

**Directions:** Divide the children into two teams and have them line up. Give the first child in each line a party hat to wear. Stand at an end point opposite the teams. Remind the children that the king in the Bible story was at a party when he got the message from God.

At your signal, the first child in each line runs to you and listens to a message that you whisper. Those children run back to their team and tell the message to their team. The first player gives the party hat to the second player, who puts it on and runs to you for another message. Give the second players a different message for them to take back to their teams. Continue play until everyone has had a chance to wear the hat and carry a message.

"Messages" you might give the children may include:

Obey God.

God loves you.

Praise only God.

God cares about you.

God listens when you pray.

Trust God for help.

## LESSON 39 SNACK:
# Popcorn Prayer Snack

**Supplies:** Popcorn, paper plates

Have the kids pray some more "popcorn" prayers to thank God for the food before distributing the snack. (See Share and Prayer.) When finished, be sure all the children help pick up any popcorn that has fallen on the floor.

## LESSON 39 ELEMENTARY GAME:
# The King's New Laws

**Supplies:** None

**Directions:** Choose one child to be the king and stand at the front of the game area. Each time a "new law" is given, the children must obey. Children who "obey" the law get to take a big step forward. The first child to touch the king gets to take over and be the new king. When a new king is "crowned," all of the kids go back to the starting line.

Laws:

Kids with blue eyes must hum the chorus of the unit song, "It Pays to Obey."

Kids wearing blue must say the Bible memory verse.

Kids shorter than me must ask God to help them obey.

Kids wearing stripes must shake hands with each other.

Kids with short hair must do five toe touches.

Kids with freckles must do five jumping jacks.

Kids with Jesus in their heart must shout, "I love You, Jesus."

## LESSON 39 PRESCHOOL GAME:
# Lion to Lion

**Supplies:** None

**Directions:** Choose one child to be IT. All the other children should be paired up. If need be, have a Park Patrol helper be a partner. When IT calls, "Lion to lion," the children have to change partners. IT tries to find a partner. Children should hold hands when they find a new partner. The extra player is the new IT.

For older children, the leader can have the children move around the room as lions. When the leader calls, "Lion to lion," the children then find a partner.

# LESSON 40 SNACK:
# Colorful Treats

**Supplies:** A multicolored snack food of your choice, such as colorful fish-shaped crackers, red and green grapes, candy-coated chocolate candies, etc.; napkins

**Directions:** Give each child a serving of the snack you chose on a napkin. As the children eat, talk about the colors in the snack and how colors can represent our feelings. You might have a Noah's Park puppet talk with the children about the colors. Remind the children that they can talk to Jesus about whatever they are feeling or experiencing.

# LESSON 40 ELEMENTARY GAME:
# Escape from Damascus

**Supplies:** Flashlights, baskets (preferably large baskets), classroom chairs

**Directions: Paul first met Jesus on the road to Damascus in a bright light that blinded him. Later he escaped from Damascus in a basket and ran to Jerusalem. In our game, we will shine a bright light and carry a basket to remind us of Paul's adventures.**

Divide the children into teams and have them line up at a starting point for a relay. At the opposite end of the playing area, set up a chair for each team and place a basket on it. Give the first player on each team a flashlight.

At your signal, the players holding the flashlights turn it on and run to their team's chair. They pick up the basket, turn off and carefully set down the flashlights, and run back to their teams. (You may want to position Park Patrol helpers by the chairs to make sure the flashlights do not roll off and break.) The players hand the basket to the second player in line, who run back to the chair and exchange the basket for the flashlight. They turn on the flashlights and run back to their teams. Continue in this manner, carrying the flashlights or baskets back and forth, until all the players on one team have had a turn to run. When a whole team is finished, they sit down and wait for the other teams to finish.

If time permits, play again.

## LESSON 40 PRESCHOOL GAME:
# Sunglass Pass

**Supplies:** Six pairs of inexpensive sunglasses

**Directions:** Have the children sit in a circle with a Park Patrol helper as the leader. The leader passes a pair of sunglasses to the child on his or her right. The children keep passing the sunglasses around the circle in the same direction. The leader introduces more pairs of sunglasses until five or six are moving around the circle in the same direction. The object is to keep the sunglasses moving without dropping any.

If you have older preschoolers, use two different colors of sunglasses. Pass one color to the right and another color to the left. Children will have to concentrate on what color is passed a certain direction.

## LESSON 41 SNACK:
# Journey Snacks

**Supplies:** Dried fruit, beef jerky or packaged beef sticks, crackers, napkins, (optional: nuts or sunflower seeds if there are no allergies)

**Directions:** Set out the food choices on trays. As the Park Patrol offers the snacks to each child, explain that people on long journeys have to take food with them that won't go bad quickly. As the children eat, talk about foods that last a long time and which ones are healthy, giving our bodies energy.

## LESSON 41 ELEMENTARY GAME:
# Walk-Ride-Sail Relay

**Supplies:** None

**Directions:** Divide children into three equally numbered teams and have them line up at a starting point. Show them where the end point is. Use a Park Patrol member where needed to help "even up numbers" in all three lines. Walk down each line for each team, giving each child a designation—walk, ride, or sail—alternating them equally for each team.

**In Bible times, people had to travel by walking, riding a donkey or horse, or sailing in a boat. If you were assigned "walk," you may walk as fast as you can to the end point and back to your team, where you tag the next player to go. If you were given "ride," you may gallop to the other end and back. If you got "sail," you must rock back and forth as you walk to the end and back.**

Be sure the children remember which action they were assigned. Then give the signal to go. The first team to finish wins. You may switch the actions among the children and play again.

## LESSON 41 PRESCHOOL GAME:
# Willing Heart Simon Says

**Supplies:** None

Have the children stand in front of you to play this variation of "Simon Says." Give the children a simple direction such as, "Wave your hand." The children should ask, "May we?" If you reply, "With willing hearts," the children can do the motion. If you don't say anything, the children should stand still. If a child accidentally does a motion, encourage him or her to listen carefully to the next direction. Keep the directions simple enough for the youngest preschooler in your class to do easily.

## LESSON 42 SNACK :
# Coin-Shaped Treats

**Supplies:** A variety of round snacks, such as crackers, carrot slices, apple or banana slices, or cookies; small plates; napkins

**Directions:** Open snack time with a prayer to thank God for the food. As the children eat, talk about the different sizes of food circles and which coins they might compare to.

If you have any treats left from Teacher Feature, you could add those to the snack time as well.

## LESSON 42 ELEMENTARY GAME:
# Roll It

**Supplies:** Nickels, washable marker, offering basket, masking tape

**Directions: Giving an offering can be fun and make us feel good. After all, we give because we love God! Let's play a game to remind us that giving can be fun.**

Mark a start line on the floor with masking tape. Place an offering basket three to five feet beyond it. Have the children line up in pairs at the start line. Demonstrate how to roll a nickel on its edge.

Give each child in the first pair a nickel. They both roll their nickels toward the offering basket, seeing which one lands the nearest. Then they retrieve the nickels and give them to the next pair of players. They also roll their nickels. Let all the children have fun rolling nickels.

If your class is large, mark start lines on two sides of the basket and let two pairs play at once. This game is not a competition, so there's no need to keep track of whose coin rolls the nearest to the basket.

Repeat as time allows.

## LESSON 42 PRESCHOOL GAME:

# Gathering Gifts Relay

**Supplies:** Two baskets, green construction paper

**Preparation:** Cut the construction paper into pieces the size of dollar bills, making three per child. Divide the "bills" into two piles at one end of your game area. Place the two baskets at the opposite end.

**Directions:** Divide the children into two equal groups. Have each group line up behind a basket.

**Let's pretend to be the people in the other country bringing money to Paul for the poor people in Jerusalem.** Have the first child in each line run to the pile of money, pick up three pieces, and run them back to put the "bills" in the basket. Repeat for each child until all have had a turn moving the "money."

## LESSON 43 SNACK:
# Pudding Power

**Supplies:** Instant pudding, milk, measuring cup, airtight plastic container for each package of pudding mix, disposable bowls, disposable spoons, napkins

**Preparation:** You may need access to a refrigerator for five minutes to let the pudding set. Check the pudding package directions.

**Directions:** Allow a few extra minutes in the lesson time for the children to prepare today's snack.

Let the children help you measure the milk and pudding mix into a container. Prepare a separate container for each box of pudding. **Now you need to use the power of your arms to mix our snack!** Be sure the lids are secure and let the children take turns shaking the pudding for the amount of time specified on the box. As they shake, discuss the "power" they are using to make this snack.

Pour the pudding into snack-size servings in disposable bowls. Your pudding mix may require refrigeration for a few minutes to set. While waiting, let the children tell about "powerful" things they know how to do. You might use a Noah's Park puppet to lead this discussion. When the pudding is ready, serve and enjoy!

## LESSON 43 ELEMENTARY GAME:
# Bubble Dodge

**Supplies:** Large container of bubble-blowing liquid, bubble wands, disposable bowls, masking tape, classroom chairs, towel for cleaning up spills

**Preparation:** Use masking tape to mark a large circle on the floor. Pour bubble liquid into bowls. Place each bowl on a chair at regular intervals around the outside of the circle.

**Directions:** Divide the class in half, and have one half stand within the circle and the other half spread out around the outside of the circle. *Warn the children not to bump the chairs or spill the bubble liquid.*

At your signal, those on the outside of the circle use a bubble wand to start "powerfully" blowing bubbles at those on the inside. The children in the circle use their "body power" to duck, jump, and dodge to avoid being hit by a bubble. The children may keep track, if they wish, of how many bubbles touched them.

After a couple of minutes, have the two groups switch places and play again. Be sure to clean up any slippery spills right away.

## LESSON 43 PRESCHOOL GAME:
# Hug Time

**Supplies:** Noah's Park Children's Church CD, CD player

**Directions:** Play the unit song, "God Wants You," from the Noah's Park CD, and have the children move around the room at random. When the music stops, each child finds someone to hug. (If you prefer the children not hug, they could link arms, give high fives, or hold hands.) While the children are hugging, they should tell their friend, "Jesus' power is for real." Play for as long as your game time allows, and encourage the children to find a different friend to hug each time.

For older preschoolers, you may ask them to make "group hugs" of three or four children at a time. You may want to consider joining the groups for your own hugs!

## LESSON 44 SNACK:
# Stick Together

**Supplies:** Sunflower seed butter, jelly, crackers, plastic knives, small plates, napkins

**Directions:** To emphasize that God is always with us, serve some foods that "stick together." Set out the supplies, and let the children make themselves mini sandwiches of sunflower seed butter and jelly. Some children may prefer to use just one spread, but that's okay since both are sticky.

As the children eat, remind them that God "sticks with them" through all circumstances.

## LESSON 44 ELEMENTARY GAME:
# Throw It Overboard!

**Supplies:** Soft foam balls or balloons, masking tape, (optional: oscillating fan and extension cord)

**Directions:** Place a line of masking tape down the center of your game area. Divide the children in half and have each group stand on one side of the line. Choose one side to be the ship and the other side to be the water. Place an equal number of balls or balloons on each side.

**When Paul's ship was in the hurricane, the men started throwing things overboard to lighten the ship. Some of you are on the ship, and you will throw the balls (balloons) overboard, or over the line, into the sea. The other half of you are waves in the sea, and you will toss the balls back into the boat, or over the line. When I say stop, we'll see which side was more successful at unloading—the boat or the sea.**

Give the signal to go, and time the game for about two minutes. If you'd like to make the game more challenging, set up a "hurricane wind" to blow the balls or balloons around—an oscillating fan aimed at the game area. When time is up, have the groups stop and count the balloons on their side. If the children still have energy left, switch sides and play again.

## LESSON 44 PRESCHOOL GAME:
# Ship in a Storm

**Supplies:** Twin or full flat sheet (or a small parachute), small foam ball

**Directions:** Spread the sheet on the floor. Space the children equally around the edges. Have the children bend down, grip the edge of the sheet with both hands, and stand up straight again.

**Paul was put in jail.** The children walk in a circle holding the sheet. Then stand still.

**Paul was put on a ship to sail to Rome.** Toss a ball onto the sheet. Have the children slightly shake their arms up and down to create waves.

**A storm came up. God kept Paul safe.** Have the children make bigger waves. Encourage them to work together to keep the ball on the sheet as long as possible.

## LESSON 45 SNACK:
# Sweet Scrolls

**Supplies:** Small-size tortillas, sweetened cheese spreads or jelly, plastic knives, plates, napkins

**Directions:** Give each child a tortilla on a plate. Let them choose a spread and use a plastic knife to spread a thin layer on their tortilla. Demonstrate how to roll up the tortilla from two sides to make a scroll. Let the children enjoy eating their sweet scrolls!

## LESSON 45 ELEMENTARY GAME:
# Scroll Search

**Supplies:** Colorful paper in two colors, cut in half

**Preparation:** Roll up each half-sheet of paper like a scroll. Use five or six for each team. (Each team has its own color.)

**Directions:** Divide the class into two groups. The first group hides the scrolls of one color in the area that you designate. Set clear boundaries so the children know where to hide the scrolls. The second group waits in a different area until all the scrolls are hidden. The second group then looks for the scrolls while the first group watches. The first group may give clues by saying, "Prophets speak loudly," when someone is near a scroll or "Prophets speak softly" when someone moves away from where a scroll is hidden.

When all the scrolls have been found, switch groups to give the "hiders" a chance to be the "searchers."

## LESSON 45 PRESCHOOL GAME:
# God's Promises

**Supplies:** None needed

**Directions:** Ask two Park Patrol helpers to stand at the far end of the room to play the role of the prophets.

**The prophets told about God's promises. Let's go hear what they have to say to us today.**

One at a time, have the children hop to the "prophets." Once a child is there, the prophets should tell him or her one of the following:

God will send a Savior.

He will come from David's family.

He will have a special name.

He will be born in Bethlehem.

Each child then skips back and repeats to the others what the prophet told him or her.

## LESSON 46 SNACK:
# Bible-Time Foods

**Supplies:** Simple breads, grape juice, dried fruits, napkins, disposable cups, (optional: margarine or cheese spread and plastic knives)

**Directions:** Give each child a slice of bread. If you have different kinds to choose from, let the children choose a small piece of each slice. Let the children try various dried fruits. Also serve grape juice.

As the children eat, explain that in Bible times it was common for people to eat bread and grape juice.

## LESSON 46 ELEMENTARY GAME:
# Gift Pyramid Relay

**Supplies:** Boxes in various sizes, at least five per team, (optional: Christmas gift wrap)

**Preparation:** If you have time, you may wrap the boxes in Christmas gift wrap.

**Directions:** Place an equal number of boxes for each team at one end of the playing area. Let Park Patrol helpers play if you don't have equal numbers. Gather the children around one set of boxes. Demonstrate how to stack the boxes into a pyramid, with the largest on the bottom. Be sure the children understand. Then mix up the boxes and return them to their spot.

Divide the children into teams of equal number. Line them up behind a starting point, each team across from a pile of boxes. At your signal, the first player lined up for each team runs to his team's pile of boxes, stacks them into a pyramid, and runs back to tag the second player. The second player runs to the boxes, unstacks them, and returns to tag the third player. That player rebuilds a pyramid from the boxes. Play until one team has had all players run and is seated. Then play again, switching places, so that all players have a chance to build.

You might warn the players who unstack the boxes to not simply knock them over or it will take their next player longer to gather them together to rebuild the team's pyramid.

# LESSON 46 PRESCHOOL GAME:
# Angel, Mary, Joseph

**Supplies:** None

**Directions:** This game is a variation on "Duck, Duck, Goose." Ask the children to sit in a circle. Choose one child to be the Angel. The child who is the Angel walks around the outside of the circle and taps the seated children on the shoulder while walking by. With each tap, the Angel says, "Mary." But when the angel taps a child and says, "Joseph," the angel takes off running and the tagged child jumps up and chases the Angel. The Angel tries to make it to the tagged child's open spot before being tagged. If the Angel succeeds, the tagged child becomes the new Angel. But if the Angel gets tagged while being chased, the same child remains the Angel.

## LESSON 47 SNACK:
# Animal Crackers

**Supplies:** Animal-shaped cookies or crackers, napkins

**Preparation:** Give a few animal treats on a napkin to each child. Let the children identify their animals and tell if they know if that animal may have been in the stable when Jesus was born (or lived in Israel during Bible times). Children may not know, but they will enjoy discussing it, and the whole nativity scene will become more real.

## LESSON 47 ELEMENTARY GAME:
# Good News Relay

**Supplies:** Newspapers, rubber bands, classroom chairs

**Preparation:** Separate newspapers into small sections. Roll up each section and secure it with a rubber band. Make one rolled newspaper for each team.

**Directions:** Divide the children into teams, and give each team a newspaper. Designate a start line, place chairs at a turnaround point.

At your signal, the first player on each team runs to the chair and pauses to yell, "Good news! Jesus is born!" Then those players run back to their teams to tag the next player to go. Play until one team has had every player go and the team is seated.

In between rounds, let the children name ways we spread news—through newspapers, e-mail, Web sites, TV, and so on.

## LESSON 47 PRESCHOOL GAME:
# Shepherds Go to Bethlehem

**Supplies:** None

**Directions:** The children form a circle and are shepherds. One child is seated in the middle. Make a goal line at one end of the game area to be Bethlehem. The shepherds walk in a circle around the seated child, counting as they walk. When you call out, "We're almost to Bethlehem," the shepherds run to the goal line. The child seated in the middle jumps up and tries to tag children before they reach Bethlehem. Children who are tagged sit in the middle of the circle for the next round and help catch travelers.

## LESSON 48 SNACK:
# Christmas Cookies

**Supplies:** Shortbread or sugar cookies; prepared icing in white, green, or red; red and green sprinkles or colored sugar; plastic knives; disposable plates; napkins

**Directions:** Give each child a plain cookie on a plate. Show the children how to spread a thin layer of icing across the cookies. The children may then decorate their "Christmas" cookies with red and green sprinkles or sugar.

As the children decorate and eat, let them share stories of favorite Christmas memories and traditions.

## LESSON 48 ELEMENTARY GAME:
# Wise Man Caravan

**Supplies:** Pillowcases of the same size (one per team), stopwatch or a watch with a second hand, one set of "traveling necessities" for each team: pillow, stuffed animal, set of pajamas, pair of slippers, tube of toothpaste, and a ball

**Preparation:** Make one pile of identical items for each team.

**Directions:** Divide the children into teams of three to five, being sure each team has the same number of children. Give each team a pillowcase.

**What do you take when you go on a long trip? Any of these things?** Point out the pile of traveling necessities. **The wise men probably didn't take these things on their journey. But we're going to help them travel anyway. Your job is to work as a team to carry all these things from the East** (point out the start line) **to Bethlehem** (point to the finish line).

**But here's the catch. You may not carry anything with your hands. And you can't put anything *inside* your team's pillowcase. You have to lay the pillowcase flat, pile everything on top, and as a team carry the pillowcase to**

Bethlehem. And everyone on the team has to have two hands holding or at least touching the pillowcase.

This is not a race against the other teams, but I will time you to see how long it takes. Each team is a camel in the caravan, so I'll stop timing when the last team reaches Bethlehem. If you drop something, you have to stop moving and put it back on the pillowcase before anyone on your team can take another step forward.

Be sure the children understand the directions. Then give the signal to begin. Let the Park Patrol give suggestions to the teams and cheer encouragement. Time how long it takes for the whole "caravan" to reach Bethlehem. If time permits, let the children mix up their items, trade some team members, and play again.

## LESSON 48 PRESCHOOL GAME:
# Follow the Star

**Supplies:** A paper star, Noah's Park puppets

**Directions:** This is a version of "Follow the Leader." Choose one child to begin as the leader, and have the children line up behind him or her. The leader should hold the star high in one hand. Have the children follow the leader and do what he or she does. Encourage the leader to move around the room while doing movements such as hopping, marching, flapping arms, clapping hands above heads, taking baby steps, and so on. The children should take turns being the leader. The children may use the puppets to do some of the movements.

## LESSON 49 SNACK:
# Never-Ending Treats

**Supplies:** Any ring-shaped snacks, such as donuts, certain chips, certain candies; napkins (Note: If hollow, ring-shaped snacks are hard to find, you may use round snacks without a hole in the middle, such as fruit slices.)

**Directions:** Give each child a handful of "eternal" treats on a napkin. Point out that they are round, like a circle, so they have no beginning and no end. **We learned at the beginning of our lesson that God is eternal—He has no beginning and no end, just like a circle. Let these treats remind you of God's gift of eternal life through Jesus.**

## LESSON 49 ELEMENTARY GAME:
# Hoop Race

**Supplies:** Large plastic hoop toys (one per team), stopwatch or watch with a second hand

**Directions:** This game needs to be played on a hard, smooth surface. Divide the children into small teams. Have each team line up at a starting point. Place a chair opposite each team about 15 feet away. Be sure there is plenty of space between chairs.

At your signal, the first player on each team rolls their hoop across the playing area, around the chair, and back to their team. If a hoop falls over or steers off course, the player simply picks it up and keeps rolling from that point. Then the next player on the team goes. Set a time limit, such as three minutes, and have the teams keep count of how many times their team can roll the hoop around the chair and back in that time. The winning team is the one with the highest number of go-rounds. As an option, let the players work in pairs to roll their team's hoop.

## LESSON 49 PRESCHOOL GAME:
# "God Loves You" Train

**Supplies:** None

**Directions:** You or a Park Patrol helper may be the leader. The leader goes up to a child and says this rhyme:

> **God loves you.**
>
> **God loves me.**
>
> **Tell me, tell me,**
>
> **What's your name?**

The child tells the leader his or her name. The leader repeats the child's name. The child then stands behind the leader, putting his or her hands on the leader's waist or shoulders, to begin a train. The leader then takes the train to another child, says the rhyme, repeats the name, and adds that child to the train. Repeat until all the children are part of the train. You may want to have the train travel a little way around the room between each repetition of the rhyme. Go all the way around the room when the train is complete.

## LESSON 50 SNACK:
# "J" Is for Jesus

**Supplies:** Crackers, squeeze cheese or squeeze cream cheese, napkins

**Directions:** Ask the children what letter the name "Jesus" begins with. When they answer "J," show them how to draw a letter J on a cracker using the squeeze cheese. Let each child prepare his or her own crackers. As the children eat, let them each tell one thing they know about Jesus.

## LESSON 50 ELEMENTARY GAME:
# Jesus Knows You

**Supplies:** Scrap paper, pencils

**Directions:** Give out paper and pencils, and encourage each child to write down a few special things about himself or herself. They may write down things like a hobby they enjoy, a place they have visited, or their favorite school subject or food. Ask the children to write down at least three things, and encourage them to choose things that not a lot of other children may do or have done. Let the Park Patrol circulate and help with writing as needed. Have each child include his or her name at the bottom.

Collect the papers and mix them up. Explain that Jesus knows all these things about the children and that soon the rest of the class will know them too! Read the items on one paper. As soon as someone wants to make a guess as to who it may be, that person jumps up. Pause to let several kids jump up. Then choose one to make a guess. Let all those standing guess until the correct person is guessed.

Then read another paper, and let the children jump up and guess again. Caution the children not to call out answers but to wait until you call on them. If you are short on time and have a big group, you could divide into two and have a Park Patrol helper lead the guessing in the other group.

## LESSON 50 PRESCHOOL GAME:
# Call-a-Name Tag

**Supplies:** None

**Directions:** Have the children spread out in your game area. Choose one child to be IT. This child tries to tag the other children, while they try to avoid being touched. Whenever someone is tagged, that child has to call out "Jesus loves ____," naming the child who tagged them. Then this child becomes the new IT and tries to tag others.

## LESSON 51 SNACK:
# Cross Creations

**Supplies:** Pretzel rods, canned squirt cheese (or sunflower seed butter and plastic knives), disposable plates, napkins, cups of water

**Directions:** Give each child two pretzel rods on a plate. Let the children squirt cheese or spread sunflower seed butter on their rods and connect them to form a cross. The children may appreciate a cup of water with this sticky snack!

## LESSON 51 ELEMENTARY GAME:
# Forgiven Tag

**Supplies:** None

**Directions:** Forgiven tag is much like freeze tag. One person (or more if your group is large) chases the rest of the children. When the tagger touches someone, he says, "You've done wrong." The tagged person kneels on the floor and waits until all the other children have been tagged. Then the tagger returns to each child, touches him, and says, "God forgives you." When everyone has been forgiven, a new game starts with a new tagger.

# LESSON 51 PRESCHOOL GAME:
# God Forgives Bridge

**Supplies:** None

**Directions:** This game is a version of the familiar children's game "London Bridge." Choose two children to be the bridge. These children face each other holding both of their partner's hands. They then raise their clasped hands to create the bridge. The rest of the children walk in a line under the bridge and circle back around again for more turns. As they walk, sing these words to the tune of "London Bridge:"

> **Jesus shows us God forgives,**
> **God forgives, God forgives.**
> **Jesus shows us God forgives.**
> **God loves (child's name).**

The children fill in the blank by singing the name of the child who is under the bridge at that moment. The two children forming the bridge drop their hands to catch that child. That child and a friend of his choosing become the new bridge for another round.

## LE... 4 52 SNACK:

# Sweet Spices

**Supplies:** Any treat made with cinnamon, cloves, and other aromatic spices, such as spice cake, gingerbread cookies, snickerdoodles, cinnamon banana bread, and so on; plates or napkins

**Directions:** Give out the treat you chose and ask the children to sniff it. See if anyone can name any of the spices in it. Many children this age can recognize cinnamon, if it is strong, but not other spices.

As the children eat, explain that spices were an important part of Bible-time culture. They were used at graves—as in today's Bible story—and also for cooking and making the home smell better.

## LESSON 52 ELEMENTARY GAME:

# Run to the Tomb

**Supplies:** Tomb picture on butcher paper used in Elementary Bible Story and Share and Prayer

**Directions:** Divide the children into teams, and have them line up across from the tomb picture. At your signal, the first player in each line runs to the tomb, bends way over to pretend to look in (you might set the rule that they have to touch their toes), and races back to their line. Before tagging the next player to go, the first player has to shout, "Jesus is alive!" Then he or she tags the second player in line, who repeats the actions. Play until everyone has had a chance to run and shout.

# LESSON 52 PRESCHOOL GAME:
# Angel Surprise

**Supplies:** Two chairs

**Directions:** Set two chairs at one end of the game area. Ask two children to sit in the chairs and be angels. The rest of the children start at the other end of your playing area. The angels close their eyes while the rest of the players try to sneak up to them. At any time, an angel can call out "Jesus is alive," open his or her eyes, and jump up to chase the children back to the start line. Any child who is tagged replaces the angel in the chair.

You may want to have a Park Patrol helper stay near the angels to help them decide when to shout and chase. (They should wait until the other players are close enough to catch.) The angels must also shout *before* they open their eyes.

## LESSON 53 SNACK:
# Cheesy Books

**Supplies:** Club crackers, individually wrapped cheese slices, plastic knives, disposable plates, napkins

**Directions:** Give each child a slice of cheese and some club crackers. The children set two rectangular pieces of cracker side by side to form the book covers. The children may use plastic knives to slice their cheese into smaller rectangles to form pages. When the covers set side by side they look like an open book.

As the children eat their "books," ask about what kinds of Bibles or Bible storybooks they use at home.

## LESSON 53 ELEMENTARY GAME:
# Obstacles on the Road to Emmaus

**Supplies:** Blindfolds

**Preparation:** Set up a very simple obstacle course using classroom tables and chairs.

**Directions:** Let the children each choose a partner. Have pairs line up at the start of the obstacle course. Blindfold one child in each of the first few pairs. Have pairs link arms.

**Jesus walked with the two men on the road to Emmaus. They saw Him, but in a sense, they didn't see Him because they didn't realize who He was.**

The first pair walks "the road to Emmaus," with the seeing child carefully leading the blindfolded child. This is not a race so they should not hurry. Once they are past the first few obstacles, signal the second pair to begin. If your course is long, you might have three or four pairs traveling at once.

# LESSON 53 PRESCHOOL GAME:
# The Emmaus Road

**Supplies:** Masking tape

**Preparation:** Using masking tape, place two lines of tape on the floor to resemble a short road.

**Directions:** Divide the children into two groups. Have one group sit facing the road, on one side of the tape. Have the other group sit facing the road on the opposite side.

**Let's pretend this is the road to Emmaus. As we go down the road, let's pretend to be Jesus' two helpers.** Ask the first child in each group to stand at one end of the road. The two children should do whatever action you decide (walk, hop, skip). They should then do the action as they go down the road together. At the end of the road, have the children run back and say, "Jesus is alive!"

Repeat until all the children have gone down the road. If you have older preschoolers, vary the action with each group of children.